LONGMAN LITERATURE SHAKESPEARE

Romeo and Juliet

William Shakespeare

Editor: Celeste Flower

Longman Literature Shakespeare
Series editor: Roy Blatchford
Consultant: Jackie Head

Macbeth　　0 582 08827 5 (paper)
　　　　　　0 582 24592 3 (cased)
Romeo and Juliet　　0 582 08836 4 (paper)
　　　　　　　　　　0 582 24591 5 (cased)
The Merchant of Venice　　0 582 08835 6 (paper)
　　　　　　　　　　　　　0 582 24593 1 (cased)
A Midsummer Night's Dream　　0 582 08833 X (paper)
　　　　　　　　　　　　　　　0 582 24590 7 (cased)
Julius Caesar　　0 582 08828 3 (paper)
　　　　　　　　0 582 24589 3 (cased)
Twelfth Night　　0 582 08834 8 (paper)
Othello　　0 582 09719 3 (paper)
King Lear　　0 582 09718 5 (paper)
Hamlet　　0 582 09720 7 (paper)

Longman Literature
Series editor: Roy Blatchford

Plays

Alan Ayckbourn　　*Absurd Person Singular*　　0582 06020 6
Arthur Miller　　*An Enemy of the People*　　0 582 09717 7
J B Priestley　　*An Inspector Calls*　　0 582 06012 5
Terence Rattigan　　*The Winslow Boy*　　0 582 06019 2
Willy Russell　　*Educating Rita*　　0 582 06013 3
　　　　　　　　Shirley Valentine　　0 582 08173 4
Peter Shaffer　　*The Royal Hunt of the Sun*　　0 582 06014 1
　　　　　　　Equus　　0 582 09712 6
Bernard Shaw　　*Arms and the Man*　　0 582 07785 0
　　　　　　　Pygmalion　　0 582 06015 X
　　　　　　　Saint Joan　　0 582 07786 9
Oscar Wilde　　*The Importance of Being Earnest*　　0 582 07784 2

Other titles in the Longman Literature series are listed on page 359.

Editorial material for Key Stage 3 (pages 343–57) prepared by Geoff Barton and John Butcher.

Contents

Introduction

Shakespeare's life and times

Shakespeare was born into a time of change. Important discoveries about the world were changing people's whole way of life, their thoughts and their beliefs. The fact that we know very little of Shakespeare's particular life story does not mean that we cannot step into his world.

What do we know about Shakespeare?

Imagine for a minute you are Shakespeare, born in 1564, the son of a businessman who is making his way in Stratford-upon-Avon. When you are thirteen, Francis Drake sets off on a dangerous sea voyage around the world, to prove that it is round, not flat, and to bring back riches. The trades people who pass in and out of your town bring with them stories of other countries, each with their own unique culture and language. You learn in school of ancient heroic myths taught through Latin and Greek, and often, to bring these stories alive, travelling theatres pass through the town acting, singing, performing, and bringing with them tales of London. But, at the age of fourteen your own world shifts a little under your feet; your father has got into serious debt, you find yourself having to grow up rather fast.

This is an unremarkable life so far — the death of your sisters is not an uncommon occurrence at this time, and even when you marry at eighteen, your bride already pregnant at the ceremony, you are not the first to live through life in this way. After your daughter, your wife gives birth to twins, a girl and a boy, one of whom dies when he is eleven. But before this, for some reason only you know, perhaps to do with some poaching you are involved in or because your marriage to a woman eight years older than you is having difficulties, you travel to London. There you eventually join the theatre, first as an actor and then as a writer. You write for the theatres in the inn yards, then for Queen Elizabeth in court, and when she dies, for King James I. As well as this you write for the large theatres which are being built in London: the Rose, the Globe, Blackfriars and the Swan. You die a rich man.

What did Shakespeare find in London?

When Shakespeare first travelled to London he found a city full of all that was best and worst in this new era of discovery. There was trade in expensive and fashionable items, a bubbling street life with street-theatre, pedlars of every sort, sellers of songs and poems. Industry was flourishing in textiles, mining, the manufacture of glass, iron, and sugar. The place to be known was the court of Queen Elizabeth. She was unmarried and drew many admirers even in her old age, maintaining a dazzling social world with her at its centre. There were writers and poets, grasping what they could of the new world, building on the literature of other countries, charting the lingering death of medieval life and the chaotic birth of something new.

By contrast, Shakespeare also found poverty, death and disease. The plague, spread by rats, found an easy home in these narrow streets, often spilling over with dirt and sewage: it killed 15,000 people in London in 1592 alone. It was an overcrowded city: the increased demand for wool for trade brought about the enclosure of land in the countryside, and this, coupled with bad harvests, brought the peasants, thrown off their land and made poor, into London to seek wealth.

What was England like in Shakespeare's day?

England was a proud nation. Elizabeth would not tolerate rivals and destroyed her enemies. In 1587 she had Mary Queen of Scots executed for treason, and in 1588 her navy defeated a huge armada of ships from Spain. Both acts were prompted by religion. In maintaining the Protestant Church of England her father, King Henry VIII, had established, Elizabeth stood out against a strong Catholic Europe. Within the Protestant religion too, there were divisions, producing extreme groups such as the Puritans who believed that much of the Elizabethan social scene was sinful, the theatres being one of their clearest targets for disapproval. Her power was threatened for other reasons too. In 1594 her doctor was executed for attempting to poison her, and in 1601 one of her favourites, the Earl of Essex, led an unsuccessful revolt against her.

When Elizabeth died in 1603 and James I succeeded her, he brought a change. He was a Scottish king, and traditionally Scotland and England had had an uneasy relationship. He was interested in witchcraft and he supported the arts, but not in the same way as Elizabeth had. He too met with treason, in the shape of Guy Fawkes and his followers, who in 1605 attempted to blow up The Houses of Parliament. If Shakespeare needed examples of life at its extremes, he had them all around him, and his closeness to the court meant he understood them more than most.

What other changes did Shakespeare see?

Towards the end of Shakespeare's life, in Italy, a man Shakespeare's age invented the telescope and looked at the stars. His radical discoveries caused him to be thrown out of the Catholic Church. For fifteen centuries people had believed in a picture of the universe as held in crystal spheres with order and beauty, and everything centring around the earth. In this belief the sun, moon and stars were the heavens; they ruled human fate, they were distant and magical. Galileo proved this was not so. So, the world was no longer flat and the earth was not the centre of the universe. It must have felt as if nothing was to be trusted anymore.

What do Shakespeare's plays show us about Elizabethan life?

Even without history books much of Shakespeare's life can be seen in his plays. They are written by one who knows of the tragedy of sudden death, and illness, and of the splendour of the life of the court in contrast to urban and rural poverty. He knows the ancient myths of the Greeks and Romans, the history of change in his own country, and, perhaps from reading the translations carried by merchants to London, he knows the literature of Spain and Italy.

His plays also contain all the hustle and bustle of normal life at the time. We see the court fool, the aristocracy, royalty, merchants and the servant classes. We hear of bear-baiting, fortune-telling, entertaining, drinking, dancing and singing. As new changes happen they are brought into the plays, in the form of maps, clocks, or the latest fashions. Shakespeare wrote to perform, and his plays were performed to bring financial reward. He studied his audience closely and produced what they wanted. Sometimes, as with the focus on witchcraft in *Macbeth* written for King James I, this was the celebration of something which fascinated them; sometimes, as with the character of Malvolio in *Twelfth Night*, it was the mockery of something they despised.

What do Shakespeare's plays tell us about life now?

You can read Shakespeare's plays to find out about Elizabethan life, but in them you will also see reflected back at you the unchanging aspects of humanity. It is as if in all that changed around him, Shakespeare looked for the things that would *not* change – like love, power, honour, friendship and loyalty – and put them to the test. In each he found strength and weakness.

We see *love*:

- at first sight,
- which is one-sided,
- between young lovers,
- in old age,
- between members of one family,
- lost and found again.

We see *power*:

- used and abused,
- in those who seek it,
- in those who protect it with loyalty,
- in the just and merciful rule of wise leaders,
- in the hands of wicked tyrants.

We see *honour*:

- in noble men and women,
- lost through foolishness,
- stolen away through trickery and disloyalty.

We see *friendship*:

- between men and men, women and women, men and women,
- between masters and servants,
- put to the test of jealousy, grief and misunderstanding.

These are just some examples of how Shakespeare explored in his plays what it was to be human. He lived for fifty-two years and wrote thirty-seven plays, as well as a great number of poems. Just in terms of output this is a remarkable achievement. What is even more remarkable is the way in which he provides a window for his audiences into all that is truly human, and it is this quality that often touches us today.

What are Comedies, Tragedies and Histories?

When Shakespeare died, his players brought together the works he has written, and had them published. Before this some of the plays had only really existed as actors' scripts written for their parts alone. Many plays in Shakespeare's day and before were not written down at all, but spoken, and kept in people's memories from generation to generation. So, making accurate copies of Shakespeare's plays was not easy and there is still some dispute over how close to the original scripts our current editions are. Ever since they were first published people have tried to make sense of them. Sometimes they are described under three headings: Comedy, Tragedy and History. The dates on the chart that follows refer to the dates of the first recorded performances or, if this is not known, the date of first publication. They may have been performed earlier but history has left us no record; dating the plays exactly is therefore difficult.

COMEDY	HISTORY	TRAGEDY
	King John (1590)	
	Henry VI, Part I (1592)	
Comedy of Errors (1594)		Titus Andronicus (1594)
The Taming of the Shrew (1594)		
Two Gentlemen of Verona (1594)		
The Merry Wives of Windsor (1597)	Richard II (1597)	Romeo and Juliet (1597)
	Richard III (1597)	
The Merchant of Venice (1598)	Henry IV, Part II (1598)	
Love's Labour's Lost (1598)		
As You Like It (1600)	Henry V (1600)	
A Midsummer Night's Dream (1600)	Henry VI, Part II (1600)	
Much Ado About Nothing (1600)	Henry VI, Part III (1600)	
Twelfth Night (1600)		
Troilus and Cressida (1601)		
		Hamlet (1602)
Measure for Measure (1604)	Henry IV, Part I (1604)	Othello (1604)
All's Well That Ends Well (1604)		

COMEDY	HISTORY	TRAGEDY
		Julius Caesar (1605)
		Macbeth (1606)
		King Lear (1606)
		Antony and Cleopatra (1608)
		Timon of Athens (1608)
		Coriolanus (1608)
Pericles (1609)		
Cymbeline (1611)		
The Winter's Tale (1611)		
The Tempest (1612)	*Henry VIII* (1612)	

Comedy = a play which maintains a thread of joy throughout and ends happily for most of its characters.

Tragedy = a play in which characters must struggle with circumstances and in which most meet death and despair.

History = a play focusing on a real event or series of events which actually happened in the past.

These three headings can be misleading. Many of the comedies have great sadness in them, and there is humour in most of the tragedies, some of which at least point to happier events in the future. Some of the tragedies, like **Macbeth** and **Julius Caesar**, make history their starting point.

We do not know exactly when each play was written but from what we know of when they were performed we can see that Shakespeare began by writing poetry, then histories and comedies. He wrote most of his tragedies in the last ten years of his life, and in his final writings wrote stories full of near-tragic problems which, by the end of the plays he resolved. Sometimes these final plays (*Pericles*, *Cymbeline*, *The Winter's Tale* and *The Tempest*) are called Comedies, sometimes they are called Romances or simply The Problem Plays.

Where were Shakespeare's plays performed?

Plays in Shakespeare's day were performed in several places, not just in specially designed theatres.

Inn Yard Theatre: Players performed in the open courtyard of Elizabethan inns. These were places where people could drink, eat and stay the night. They were popular places to make a break in a journey and to change or rest horses. Some inns built a permanent platform in the yard, and the audience could stand in the yard itself, or under shelter in the galleries which overlooked the yard. The audiences were lively and used to the active entertainment of bear-baiting, cock-fighting, wrestling and juggling. Plays performed here needed to be action-packed and appealing to a wide audience. In 1574 new regulations were made to control performances in response to the number of fights which regularly broke out in the audience.

Private House Theatre: The rich lords of Elizabethan times would pay travelling theatre companies to play in the large rooms of their own private houses for the benefit of their friends. There was no stage and the audience were all seated. Torches and candles were used to create artificial lighting. Costumes played an important part in creating atmosphere but there were no sets.

Public Hall Theatre: Some town councils would allow performances of plays in their grand halls and council buildings. As well as this, ceremonial halls such as the Queen's courts in Whitehall were frequently used in this way, as were halls at Hampton Court, Richmond and Greenwich Palace. For these performances, designed for a larger audience than those given in private houses, scaffolding would be arranged for tiered seating which would sur-round a central acting area. Audiences were limited to hose with a high social standing.

Public Theatres: Unlike Public Hall theatres, these theatres were built for the purpose of presenting plays. At the end of the sixteenth century there were about 200,000 people living in London, and eleven public theatres showing performances. Of these, about half a dozen were so large that they seated about 2,000 people. The audiences, who were drawn from all sections of society, paid to see performances which began at 2 p.m. The audience sat in covered galleries around a circular acting area which was open air. Whilst the theatres stood within the City of London they were subject to its laws. They could not perform during times of worship, and they were closed during outbreaks of the plague. Theatres were often the scenes of fighting and because of the trouble this caused, in 1596 performances of plays were forbidden within the city boundaries. So people started building theatres outside the city on the south side of the River Thames.

What were the performances like?

To some extent this depended on the play being performed and the audience watching. A play performed before the court of the queen or king would need to be one that did not offend the ruler. Plays performed in the inn yard or the public theatres needed to have a wide appeal and several distractions such as dancing and music to keep the audience's attention.

Wherever they performed, the players had to create the illusion that the whole world could be seen inside their play. They had no sets, except in some cases tapestries which were hung up to show changes in scenery, but they did have bright costumes in which to perform. Scenes of battle or shipwreck were suggested by words rather than special effects, though we do know that they used burning torches, as it was due to a fire caused by one of these that the first Globe Theatre burnt down during a performance in 1613.

Actors joined together in companies, who would perform several different plays, and be sponsored by the nobility. Shakespeare became a key member of the Lord Chamberlain's company which Queen Elizabeth sponsored, and which went on to be called The King's Men when James I became king.

There were no women on the Elizabethan stage. Most female characters would be played by boys whose voices had not yet broken, or if it was an old character, by men in the company. Actors carried a reputation for being immoral and ungodly people, and were therefore thought unsuitable company for women. The men of Shakespeare's company became famous for playing particular types of characters such as the fool, the lover or the villain. Shakespeare probably created many of his parts with particular actors in mind.

Where can I find out more about Shakespeare?

Shakespeare is perhaps the world's most famous playwright and there is no shortage of books written about him. In your library or bookshop you will find books which look at:

- Shakespeare's life;
- the history of England under the reign of Queen Elizabeth I and James I;
- European history, art and literature of the sixteenth and seventeenth century;
- discoveries made throughout the world during Elizabethan times;
- characters, themes and ideas in Shakespeare's writing.

In Stratford-upon-Avon, where Shakespeare was born you can visit his birthplace, and much of the town consists of buildings which would have stood in Shakespeare's day. In addition to this there are many museums and exhibitions which tell more about Shakespeare's life and work.

Some theatrical companies today, such as the Royal Shakespeare Company, devote themselves to performing Shakespeare's plays in London, Stratford, and on tour around the country. They are always seeking new ways to bring the plays to life. However, perhaps the best way to find out more about Shakespeare is to study his plays by reading and acting them yourself and by seeing them in performance. Shakespeare wrote about what he knew, and the key to discovering how his mind and emotions worked is to look at what he wrote.

Shakespeare's language

Speaking Shakespeare

Romeo and Juliet is not a prose story but a play, and it is important that as well as reading the words you should hear them spoken. Speaking the lines is not easy at first, but with practice you should soon become better at it.

Below are some extracts from the play to get you started. Remember:

- Pause at commas, semi-colons and colons.
- Take a breath at the end of sentences, that is, where the full stops are and *not* where the lines end.
- Try to follow the meaning of the words and place the emphasis on appropriate words in order to get the meaning across.
- Try to read at a normal speaking pace: not too quickly or too slowly.
- Don't worry if you make mistakes; everyone does!

Angry words

Here are some phrases from different sections of the play. Can you get these insults and challenges to sound right?

TYBALT

What, drawn, and talk of peace? I hate the word
As I hate hell, all Montagues, and thee.
Have at thee, coward!

(Act 1, scene 1, lines 67–9)

MERCUTIO

Tybalt, you rat-catcher, will you walk?

(Act 3, scene 1, line 74)

JULIET

Blistered be thy tongue
For such a wish!

(Act 3, scene 2, lines 90–1)

CAPULET

Out, you green-sickness carrion! out, you baggage!
You tallow-face.

(Act 3, scene 5, lines 155–6)

Loving words

Romeo and Juliet declare their love for one another in the famous balcony scene. All of this takes place in secret and they are in danger of being found out all the time. Juliet is afraid that this is all too good to be true. How will you deliver the lines?

ROMEO
    Lady, by yonder blessèd moon I vow,
    That tips with silver all these fruit-tree tops –
JULIET
    O swear not by the moon, th' inconstant moon,
    That monthly changes in her circled orb,
    Lest that thy love prove likewise variable.
ROMEO
    What shall I swear by?
JULIET
                Do not swear at all;
    Or if thou wilt, swear by thy gracious self,
    Which is the god of my idolatry,
    And I'll believe thee.
ROMEO
                If my heart's dear love –
JULIET
    Well, do not swear. Although I joy in thee,
    I have no joy of this contract tonight:
    It is too rash, too unadvised, too sudden,
    Too like the lightning, which doth cease to be
    Ere one can say "It lightens".

                        (Act 2, scene 2, lines 107–20)

Word-play

In Shakespeare, words that sound the same but have different meanings (*homophones*) are often put to good comic use in puns. The play begins with just such foolery.

SAMPSON
    Gregory, on my word, we'll not carry coals.

GREGORY
    No, for then we should be colliers.

SAMPSON
> I mean, and we be in choler, we'll draw.

GREGORY
> Ay, while you live, draw your neck out of collar.

> (Act 1, scene 1, lines 1–4)

Mercutio who is a great joker, cannot resist a final pun even as he dies.

MERCUTIO
> Ask for me to-morrow and you shall find me a grave man.

> (Act 3, scene 1, line 97)

Private words

Some of the most famous lines from Shakespeare's plays come from the long speeches which characters make when they are alone on stage, reflecting on their thoughts or the events of the play. These are called soliloquies. Here is part of Juliet's soliloquy as she thinks over the possible consequences of taking a sleeping potion, which will make her appear dead.

> What if this mixture do not work at all?
> Shall I be married then to-morrow morning?
> No, no. This shall forbid it. (*She lays down her knife*)
>   Lie thou there.
> What if it be a poison which the Friar
> Subtly hath ministered to have me dead,
> Lest in this marriage he should be dishonoured
> Because he married me before to Romeo?
> I fear it is; and yet methinks it should not,
> For he hath still been tried a holy man.
> How if, when I am laid into the tomb,
> I wake before the time that Romeo
> Come to redeem me? There's a fearful point!
> Shall I not then be stifled in the vault,
> To whose foul mouth no healthsome air breathes in,
> And there die strangled ere my Romeo comes?

> (Act 4, scene 3, lines 21–35)

Prose, rhyme, blank verse

All Shakespeare's plays contain a mixture of PROSE (ordinary written language), and VERSE which may or may not rhyme. Verse which does not rhyme is called BLANK VERSE, and usually has ten beats to each line. In the first scene of *Romeo and Juliet*, Prince Escalus breaks up a street fight in the square of Verona. He speaks in blank verse. Try reading the lines out loud a few times and get a partner to count the number of syllables in each line:

Rebellious subjects, enemies to peace,	1
Profaners of this neighbour-stainèd steel –	2
Will they not hear? What ho! you men, you beasts,	3
That quench the fire of your pernicious rage	4
With purple fountains issuing from your veins,	5
On pain of torture, from those bloody hands	6
Throw your mistempered weapons to the ground,	7
And hear the sentence of your movèd Prince.	8

You will notice that in line 2 the word 'stainèd' carries a stress mark over the 'e'. In order to make line 2 fit the pattern of syllables this 'e' has to be pronounced. The same thing happens in line 8. If Shakespeare had not wanted the extra syllable to be sounded he would have left the stress mark out as in 'mistempered', line 7, or even shortened the word by using an apostrophe (in other words it could have been written 'mistemper'd'). You will also notice that 'ions' (rebell*ions*) has to be pronounced 'yns' rather than sounding the 'i' as a separate syllable. When these two pronunciations are taken into account, the ten lines have a regular number of syllables.

Blank verse is very flexible. It sounds almost like normal speech but it gives the words a musical and refined quality. For this reason it is often the nobility in Shakespeare's plays who speak in blank verse, and the servant classes who speak in prose.

In *Romeo and Juliet* the Nurse's language is very down to earth when she speaks in prose:

> Even or odd, of all the days in the year come Lammas-Eve at night shall she be
> fourteen. Susan and she – God rest all Christian souls – were of an age. Well,
> Susan is with God; she was too good for me. But, as I said, on Lammas-Eve at

night shall she be fourteen; that shall she, marry; I remember it well. 'T is since the earthquake now eleven years, and she was weaned – I never shall forget it – of all the days of the year, upon that day;

(Act 1, scene 3, lines 18–26)

In contrast to this example, Friar Lawrence speaks in rhymed verse at the start of Act 2, scene 3 and in other parts of the play

The grey-eyed morn smiles on the frowning night,
Check'ring the eastern clouds with streaks of light;
And fleckled darkness like a drunkard reels
From forth day's path and Titan's fiery wheels.

As you read the play, take note of:

- which characters normally speak in verse and which in prose;
- what circumstances cause characters to change their normal speech form.

Look carefully at the Prologues to Acts 1 and 2. These lines could if necessary stand alone as fourteen-line poems (*sonnets*). By looking at the patterns in the rhymes work out the rhyme scheme of the Shakespearean sonnet. Notice that Shakespeare uses poetic forms such as these to comment on or narrate action, or in moments of heightened emotion.

Images

You will have seen from the extracts you have already read, that Shakespeare packs a great deal of meaning into each line. He often makes a character tell us about something in such a way that we can imagine that we are looking at a painting. Many of these pictures are formed by the use of *figurative* language such as similes and metaphors.

Juliet is waiting for Romeo to come to her room on their wedding night. We know that he can only come under cover of dark and Juliet is growing impatient to see him and for night to fall. She paints a picture with a *simile* comparing her own impatience to a child's excitement. You can spot similes easily because the words 'like' or 'as' are used to make a comparison:

> So tedious is this day
>
> As is the night before some festival
> To an impatient child that hath new robes
> And may not wear them.

(Act 3, scene 2, lines 28–31)

A *metaphor* is a compressed comparison of two things which does not use the works 'like' or 'as'. Instead, one thing is described as if it *were* the other. In Act 1, scene 3, lines 79–86 Juliet's mother is telling Juliet all about the merits of Paris, who has asked for her hand in marriage. She describes Paris as if he were a beautifully made book: the book needs only a cover to complete it and Paris needs only a wife to complete his happiness:

> Read o'er the volume of young Paris' face,
> And find delight writ there with beauty's pen;
> Examine every married lineament,
> And see how one another lends content;
> And what obscured in this fair volume lies,
> Find written in the margent of his eyes.
> This precious book of love, this unbound lover,
> To beautify him, only lacks a cover.

At times Shakespeare takes the metaphor a step further. He may describe a concept or abstract idea as if it were human. This is known as *personification*. Look out for the many examples in the text; here is one to start you off. Capulet describes death as if he were the lover of Juliet:

> O son, the night before thy wedding day
> Hath Death lain with thy wife. There she lies,
> Flower as she was, defloweèd by him.
> Death is my son-in-law, Death is my heir;
> My daughter he hath wedded. I will die
> And leave him all.

(Act 4, scene 5, lines 35–40)

Courtly language

When we first meet Romeo he tells Benvolio that he is in love with Rosaline, but it is hard to believe that he is really sincere about this love because he speaks of it in the language of courtly love, a literary style rather than a means of genuine expression:

> Why then, O brawling love, O loving hate,
> O anything of nothing first create,
> O heavy lightness, serious vanity,
> Misshapen chaos of well-seeming forms,
> Feather of lead, bright smoke, cold fire, sick health,
> Still-waking sleep that is not what it is,
> This love feel I, that feel no love in this.

(Act 1, scene 1, lines 174–80)

Romeo and Juliet is a play of contrasts: darkness and light, age and youth, hatred and love. Within all these ideas there are many varieties. Love, for instance, can take many forms; desire, adoration, infatuation and so on.

Within the speech above there is a whole catalogue of opposites and contradictory ideas which we call *oxymorons*. Romeo is not the only character to use oxymoron. Look out for it in others.

Understanding the play

The practice extracts will have helped you to see how the language of the play is spoken. Speaking the words correctly and looking out for figurative language will also help you to understand what each speech means.

Here are some more ways to work out the meaning of words and phrases:

- Are the words similar to modern words and could this help you make an educated guess at their meaning? Check the glossary for words that are new to you.

- Is there a general theme in the speech or conversation which you can connect? Always read around the word or phrase to understand it in context.

- Where and when is this scene taking place? What has gone before and what is the main action? Always think about the context of the lines within plot and setting.

- What do you already know about the character? When they last appeared were they funny, sad, afraid, serious? Can you predict what sort of things this person might say and the sort of tone they might adopt?

Don't worry if you don't understand every word. On your first reading, or hearing, what is important is getting the gist of what is being said. Shakespeare's language is very rich in its ideas and images. You don't need to understand it all at once because you can enjoy finding out more each time you revisit it.

The glossary: a word of warning

The glossary has been compiled to help you understand the language of the play. On occasions complex and beautiful poetry has been translated or paraphrased into mundane, straightforward prose. When this happens, some of the original meaning is bound to be lost. You are advised, therefore, to use the glossary as a help with your first reading, but once you feel you have the main gist of the meaning, you should try to rely on it less.

Romeo and Juliet

CHARACTERS
in the play

ESCALUS, *Prince of Verona*
PARIS, *a young Count, the Prince's kinsman*
MONTAGUE
CAPULET } *heads of two families at enmity with each other*
AN OLD MAN, *Capulet's kinsman*
ROMEO, *Montague's son*
MERCUTIO, *the Prince's kinsman and Romeo's friend*
BENVOLIO, *Montague's nephew and Romeo's friend*
TYBALT, *Lady Capulet's nephew*
FRIAR LAWRENCE
FRIAR JOHN } *members of the Franciscan Order*
BALTHASAR, *Romeo's servant*
SAMPSON
GREGORY } *Capulet's servants*
A CLOWN
PETER, *servant of Juliet's Nurse*
ABRAHAM, *Montague's servant*
AN APOTHECARY
Page to Paris

LADY MONTAGUE, *Montague's wife*
LADY CAPULET, *Capulet's wife*
JULIET, *Capulet's daughter*
NURSE to Juliet

Chorus
Kinsmen of Both Families, Musicians, Guests, City
 Officers, Watchmen, Citizens, Servants and Atten-
 dants

The scenes are laid in the Italian cities of Verona and Mantua.

3

*Mercutio in the Oxford Nutshell production of **Romeo and Juliet**, 1986.*

Act 1: summary

Servants of the Montague and Capulet families meet in the city of Verona and a violent fight breaks out, the third one in recent times. Only Prince Escalus can stop it and he threatens severe penalties if such a brawl should happen again. Romeo's parents, Lord and Lady Montague, whilst pleased that he was not involved are nevertheless worried that he spends so much of his time moping. Benvolio discovers that Romeo is unhappy because Rosaline does not return his love.

Meanwhile, Lord Capulet all but promises the hand of his daughter, Juliet, to Paris and then invites him to a masked ball that evening. The servant sent out to invite the guests cannot read the list he has been given. When Romeo and Benvolio help him out they decide to attend the ball, uninvited, because Rosaline will be there.

Juliet's mother tells her to think of Paris as a most suitable potential husband, and Juliet is happy to do as her parents wish at this point.

Later that day, Romeo and his friends, including the dashing Mercutio, dance and joke on their way to the ball. All are wearing masks which help to conceal their identities. Nevertheless, Tybalt, Lady Capulet's nephew, recognises Romeo but Lord Capulet insists that there should be no more trouble in his house. Romeo and Juliet meet for the first time and instantly fall in love. Only as the revellers leave do they discover that they have given their hearts to sworn enemies of their families.

CHORUS   in Greek drama, a group of people who narrated parts of the action or commented on it between scenes. Here Shakespeare uses a single character and the prologue is written in the form of a sonnet (see Shakespeare's language, page xix).

1   *alike in dignity*   as noble as one another.

3   *ancient grudge*   old or long-term hatred.

  mutiny   disorder, riot, violence.

4   *civil*   citizens'.

5   *fatal*   lethal, bound to lead to death.

6   *star-crossed*   ill-fated. Many people believed that their fate was determined by the stars, a recurring theme in the play.

  take their life   in two senses: a) the lovers are born and b) they commit suicide, taking their own lives.

7   *misadventured piteous overthrows*   unfortunate, sad accidents.

8   *strife*   quarrelling, conflict.

9   *fearful passage*   terrible course; this begins an image of a treacherous sea-crossing continued in the line.

  death-marked   doomed to death: the navigator's mark kept him on course.

11   *but*   apart from.

  nought   nothing.

12   *two hours' traffic of our stage*   length of time the play will take to perform.

13   *attend*   listen, pay attention to

14   *What here...mend*   what I have omitted in the prologue our acting will attempt to complete.

Prologue

CHORUS
Two households, both alike in dignity,
   In fair Verona where we lay our scene,
From ancient grudge break to new mutiny,
   Where civil blood makes civil hands unclean,
From forth the fatal loins of these two foes   5
   A pair of star-crossed lovers take their life;
Whose misadventured piteous overthrows
   Doth with their death bury their parent's strife.
The fearful passage of their death-marked love,
   And the continuance of their parents' rage,   10
Which, but their children's end, nought could remove,
   Is now the two hours' traffic of our stage;
The which, if you with patient ears attend,
   What here shall miss, our toil shall strive to mend.

Exit

bucklers small shields.

1 *we'll not carry coals* we won't be treated like the humblest servants (who would have had to carry coals).

2 *colliers* coal miners, considered to be very low on the social scale.

3 *and we be...draw* if we are angry ('in choler') we'll draw our swords.
    Shakespeare is playing on the sounds of the words ('colliers', 'choler', 'collar').
    This type of word-game, called punning, was very popular with the Elizabethans.

4 *collar* hangman's noose.

5 *moved* moved to anger.

6 *thou art...to strike* you are not easily roused to hit out. This line begins another series of puns on the word 'move'.

7 *of the house* of the family (or serving them).

8 *To move...to stand* moving means changing your position, and to be brave one must stand and fight.

9 *if thou art...runn'st away* if you get the chance you'll run away.

10 *move* give me reason.

    stand as in line 8 but with a sexual connotation too, to become sexually aroused.

11 *take the wall* in Shakespeare's time all rubbish was thrown into a gutter which ran down the middle of the street. To avoid this you would walk as near to the walls of the buildings as possible. Sampson implies that he will force the Montagues to walk in the gutter if he has to pass them in the street.

Act One

Scene one

A street in Verona.

Enter SAMPSON *and* GREGORY, *servants of the Capulet household, armed with swords and bucklers.*

SAMPSON
Gregory, on my word, we'll not carry coals.

GREGORY
No, for then we should be colliers.

SAMPSON
I mean, and we be in choler, we'll draw.

GREGORY
Ay, while you live, draw your neck out of collar.

SAMPSON
I strike quickly, being moved.   5

GREGORY
But thou art not quickly moved to strike.

SAMPSON
A dog of the house of Montague moves me.

GREGORY
To move is to stir, and to be valiant is to stand:
therefore, if thou art moved thou runn'st away.

SAMPSON
A dog of that house shall move me to stand: I will   10
take the wall of any man or maid of Montague's.

12–3 *goes to the wall* proverb which means that the weak and useless are thrown aside by the strong.

15–7 *ever thrust...to the wall* Sampson is crudely suggesting that because women are weak it is easy to take sexual advantage of them. It would also be an insult to the Montagues to treat their women as common sluts.

20 *'T is all one* it's the same thing.

21 *be civil* be nice to.

24 *maidenheads* virginity.

25 *take it...wilt* take it to mean what you want it to.

26 *sense* another pun – in this line sense is used to mean *feeling* rather than *meaning* (as in line 25).

27 *able to stand* Sampson is warming to the innuendo of the conversation – already lines 8–10 have suggested sexual arousal.

28 *a pretty piece of flesh* Sampson is now boasting about his sexuality.

29–30 *'T is well...poor John* it's a good thing you're not a fish, because if you were you would be a dried hake ('poor John'), in other words, not very good quality. Gregory is suggesting that quality is better than quantity, going along with Sampson in his dirty joke.

30 *Draw thy tool* draw your weapon (but as Sampson and Gregory have been making comparison between fighting and having sex, there is also a suggestion that he needs to be sexually prepared).

GREGORY

That shows thee a weak slave, for the weakest goes
to the wall.

SAMPSON

'Tis true, and therefore women, being the weaker
vessels, are ever thrust to the wall: therefore I will 15
push Montague's men from the wall, and thrust his
maids to the wall.

GREGORY

The quarrel is between our masters, and us their
men.

SAMPSON

'T is all one. I will show myself a tyrant: when I have 20
fought with the men, I will be civil with the maids; I
will cut off their heads.

GREGORY

The heads of the maids?

SAMPSON

Ay, the heads of the maids, or their maidenheads;
take it in what sense thou wilt. 25

GREGORY

They must take it in sense that feel it.

SAMPSON

Me they shall feel while I am able to stand; and 't is
known I am a pretty piece of flesh.

GREGORY

'T is well thou art not fish; if thou hadst, thou hadst
been poor John. Draw thy tool: here comes two of 30
the house of Montagues.

32 *back*   support, be behind.

34 *Fear me not*   don't worry, I won't let you down.

35 *No, marry; I fear thee!*   By the Virgin Mary (a mild swear word), I'm afraid you
       will.

36 *take the law of our sides*   keep on the right side of the law.

38 *list*   like.

39 *bite my thumb*   an insulting sign.

40 *bear it*   put up with it.

Enter ABRAHAM *and another* SERVANT, *both of the Montague household.*

SAMPSON
My naked weapon is out. Quarrel; I will back thee.

GREGORY
How? Turn thy back and run?

SAMPSON
Fear me not.

GREGORY
No, marry; I fear thee!   35

SAMPSON
Let us take the law of our sides; let them begin.

GREGORY
I will frown as I pass by, and let them take it as they list.

SAMPSON
Nay, as they dare. I will bite my thumb at them,
which is disgrace to them if they bear it.   40

ABRAHAM
Do you bite your thumb at us, sir?

SAMPSON
I do bite my thumb, sir.

ABRAHAM
Do you bite your thumb at us, sir?

SAMPSON
(*Aside to* GREGORY) Is the law of our side if I say
"Ay"?   45

GREGORY
(*Aside to* SAMPSON) No.

51 *I am for you*   I challenge you.

55–6 *Say 'Better'*   Gregory's courage grows as another Capulet appears.

50–60 *swashing blow*   slashing stroke in fencing.

SAMPSON
(*Replying to* ABRAHAM) No, sir, I do not bite my
thumb at you, sir, but I bite my thumb, sir.

GREGORY
Do you quarrel, sir?

ABRAHAM
Quarrel sir? No, sir.   50

SAMPSON
But if you do, sir, I am for you. I serve as good a
man as you.

ABRAHAM
No better?

SAMPSON
Well, sir –

Enter BENVOLIO.

GREGORY
(*Interrupting* SAMPSON *as he sees* TYBALT *approaching*) Say 55
"Better"; here comes one of my master's kinsmen.

SAMPSON
(*To* ABRAHAM) Yes, better, sir.

ABRAHAM
You lie.

SAMPSON
Draw, if you be men. Gregory, remember thy swashing
blow.   60

(*They fight*) BENVOLIO *draws his sword and tries to separate them.*

BENVOLIO
Part, fools!

63 *art thou...heartless hinds?* have you joined in the fight with these cowards? ('heartless': without a heart or courage and also a pun on hart or male deer; 'hinds' are female deer).

66 *manage* make use of.

60 *Have at thee!* on guard! Prepare to fight!

70 *bills* spears or halberds.

partisans long spears.

73 *crutch* Lady Capulet mocks her husband – he is too old to fight and ought to walk with crutches rather than consider fighting with swords.

75 *in spite of* mocking.

Put up your swords; you know not what you do.

Enter TYBALT.

TYBALT

What, art thou drawn among these heartless hinds?
Turn thee, Benvolio; look upon thy death.

BENVOLIO

I do but keep the peace. Put up thy sword   65
Or manage it to part these men with me.

TYBALT

What, drawn, and talk of peace? I hate the word
As I hate hell, all Montagues, and thee.
Have at thee, coward!

They fight.
Enter an OFFICER *with three or four armed* CITIZENS.

OFFICER

Clubs, bills and partisans, strike! Beat them down! 70
Down with the Capulets! Down with the Montagues!

Enter CAPULET *in his nightgown, with* LADY CAPULET, *his wife.*

CAPULET

What noise is this? Give me my long sword, ho!

LADY CAPULET

A crutch, a crutch! Why call you for a sword?

CAPULET

My sword I say! Old Montague is come,
And flourishes his blade in spite of me.   75

Enter MONTAGUE *and* LADY MONTAGUE, *his wife.*

MONTAGUE

Thou villain, Capulet. (*To his wife*) Hold me not;
let me go.

17

78   *Thou shalt...a foe*   you won't move an inch to look for an enemy.

80   *Profaners...neighbour-stainèd steel*   abusers of blades covered with the blood of neighbours.

83   *pernicious*   harmful.

84   *purple fountains*   fountains of blood.

85   *mistempered*   badly made (because they are used for a harmful purpose); also a pun meaning used by people in bad tempers.

86   *sentence*   orders.

     movèd   angry (see note to line 6).

87   *civil brawls...word*   public fights started by an insignificant remark.

91   *Cast by...ornaments*   throw off their serious and respectable ways.

93   *Cankered...cankered*   rusty...evil.

95   *Your lives shall pay the forfeit*   the penalty will be your lives.

99   *our farther pleasure*   what I wish to be done (Escalus uses the royal plural).

101   *pain*   penalty.

LADY MONTAGUE
  Thou shalt not stir one foot to seek a foe.

Enter PRINCE ESCALUS *with his train.*

PRINCE
  Rebellious subjects, enemies to peace,
  Profaners of this neighbour-stainèd steel –   80
  Will they not hear? What ho! you men, you
      beasts,
  That quench the fire of your pernicious rage
  With purple fountains issuing from your veins,
  On pain of torture, from those bloody hands
  Throw your mistempered weapons to the ground,   85
  And hear the sentence of your movèd Prince.
  Three civil brawls bred of an airy word
  By thee, old Capulet, and Montague,
  Have thrice disturbed the quiet of our streets,
  And made Verona's ancient citizens   90
  Cast by their grave beseeming ornaments
  To wield old partisans in hands as old,
  Cankered with peace, to part your cankered hate.
  If ever you disturb our streets again,
  Your lives shall pay the forfeit of the peace.   95
  For this time, all the rest depart away.
  You, Capulet, shall go along with me,
  And Montague, come you this afternoon,
  To know our farther pleasure in this case,
  To old Freetown, our common judgement-
      place.   100
  Once more, on pain of death, all men depart.

                 Exeunt all except MONTAGUE, LADY MONTAGUE *and*
                                              BENVOLIO

102 *Who set...new abroach?* who started this fight? (reopened the old wound).

103 *by* here.

104 *adversary* enemy.

105 *ere* before, as.

106 *in the instant* at that moment.

108 *breathed defiance to my ears* taunted me.

109–10 *He swung...in scorn* Tybalt swung his sword round and round making the air hiss but not touching anything. An empty gesture.

112 *part and part* one side or the other.

113 *either part* both sides.

115 *fray* disturbance, fight.

118 *abroad* outside, around.

120 *That westward...city side* that is found growing in the west of the city.

122 *made* went.

ware aware.

123 *stole into the covert* crept into the shadows so as not to be seen.

124–5 *I, measuring...be found* Benvolio realises that Romeo wants to be alone because that is how he feels at the time, too.

127 *Pursued...his* did as he would want, because it was what I wanted too.

128 *gladly shunned* happily avoided.

MONTAGUE
  Who set this ancient quarrel new abroach?
  Speak, nephew. Were you by when it began?

BENVOLIO
  Here were the servants of your adversary
  And yours, close fighting ere I did approach.   105
  I drew to part them; in the instant came
  The fiery Tybalt, with his sword prepared,
  Which, as he breathed defiance to my ears,
  He swung about his head and cut the winds,
  Who, nothing hurt withal, hissed him in scorn.   110
  While we were interchanging thrusts and blows,
  Came more and more, and fought on part and part,
  Till the Prince came, who parted either part.

LADY MONTAGUE
  O where is Romeo? Saw you him to-day?
  Right glad I am he was not at this fray.   115

BENVOLIO
  Madam, an hour before the worshipped sun
  Peered forth the golden window of the east,
  A troubled mind drive me to walk abroad,
  Where, underneath the grove of sycamore
  That westward rooteth from this city side,   120
  So early walking did I see your son.
  Towards him I made, but he was ware of me,
  And stole into the covert of the wood.
  I, measuring his affections by my own,
  Which then most sought where most might not be
     found,   125
  Being one too many by my weary self,
  Pursued my humour not pursuing his,
  And gladly shunned who gladly fled from me.

130 *augmenting*   adding to.

134 *Aurora*   goddess of the dawn in Roman mythology.

135 *heavy*   sad.

136 *pens himself*   shuts himself up.

139 *portentous*   ill-omened.

    humour   mood.

140 *Unless good...remove*   unless we can give him some good advice to help him get over it.

143 *importuned*   asked.

145 *his own affections' counsellor*   will not speak to anyone about it.

147 *close*   quiet.

148 *So far from sounding and discovery*   so difficult to question.

150 *Ere*   before.

152 *from whence his sorrows grow*   where his sadness comes from.

153 *as willingly give cure as know*   be just as keen to help him get over his sadness as to know what causes it.

MONTAGUE

    Many a morning hath he there been seen,
    With tears augmenting the fresh morning's dew,   130
    Adding to clouds more clouds with his deep sighs;
    But all so soon as the all-cheering sun
    Should in the farthest east begin to draw
    The shady curtains from Aurora's bed,
    Away from light steals home my heavy son,   135
    And private in his chamber pens himself,
    Shuts up his windows, locks fair daylight out,
    And makes himself an artificial night.
    Black and portentous must this humour prove,
    Unless good counsel may the cause remove.   140

BENVOLIO

    My noble uncle, do you know the cause?

MONTAGUE

    I neither know it, nor can learn of him.

BENVOLIO

    Have you importuned him by any means?

MONTAGUE

    Both by myself and many other friends:
    But he, his own affections' counsellor,   145
    Is to himself – I will not say how true –
    But to himself so secret and so close,
    So far from sounding and discovery
    As is the bud bit with an envious worm
    Ere he can spread his sweet leaves to the air,   150
    Or dedicate his beauty to the same.
    Could we but learn from whence his sorrows
      grow,
    We would as willingly give cure as know.

155 *I'll know...denied*   I'll find out what's wrong with him unless he obstinately refuses to tell me.

156–7 *I would...true shrift*   I hope you are successful in getting him to tell you the truth about it.

158 *Good morrow*   good morning.

159 *But new-struck nine*   just past nine o'clock.

160 *hence*   from here.

Enter ROMEO.

BENVOLIO
See where he comes. So please you, step aside;
I'll know his grievance or be much denied.   155

MONTAGUE
I would thou wert so happy by thy stay
To hear true shrift. Come, madam, let's away.

Exeunt MONTAGUE *and* LADY MONTAGUE

BENVOLIO
Good morrow, cousin.

ROMEO
                              Is the day so young?

BENVOLIO
But new-struck nine.

ROMEO
                              Ay me, sad hours seem long.
Was that my father that went hence so fast?   160

BENVOLIO
It was. What sadness lengthens Romeo's hours?

ROMEO
Not having that which, having, makes them
    short.

BENVOLIO
In love?

ROMEO
Out –

BENVOLIO
Of love?   165

166   *Out of her favour*   not loved in return.

167–8   *Alas...rough in proof*   what a pity that love, which looks as if it is sweet and gentle is, in reality, a rough and demanding master.

169–70   *whose view is muffled...his will*   even though blind, Love still gets his own way. (Cupid, the son of Venus, the goddess of love, is usually depicted as blind but he still manages to hit his targets with his arrows of love.)

171   *fray*   see note to line 115.

172   *heard it all*   heard it all before.

173   *more with love*   Romeo suggests that the brawlers actually enjoyed the fight. His next few lines use the language of the courtly lover which traditionally included lots of contradictions or oxymorons (see Shakespeare's language, pages xx–xxi).

175   *create*   created.

177   *well-seeming forms*   things which appear to be good.

179   *Still-waking*   always awake.

181   *coz*   can mean cousin – in this case Benvolio is – or just kinsman, relative.

182   *oppression*   unhappiness.

183   *such is love's transgression*   this is the sin all love is guilty of; in other words this is what being in love does to you.

185–6   *Which thou wilt...of thine*   you will make my sadness grow if you force me to listen to your problems.

ROMEO

Out of her favour where I am in love.

BENVOLIO

Alas, that Love, so gentle in his view,
Should be so tyrannous and rough in proof.

ROMEO

Alas, that Love, whose view is muffled still,
Should without eyes see pathways to his will.   170
Where shall we dine? O me! What fray was here?
Yet tell me not, for I have heard it all.
Here's much to do with hate, but more with love.
Why then, O brawling love, O loving hate,
O anything of nothing first create,   175
O heavy lightness, serious vanity,
Misshapen chaos of well-seeming forms,
Feather of lead, bright smoke, cold fire, sick health,
Still-waking sleep that is not what it is,
This love feel I, that feel no love in this.   180
Dost thou not laugh?

BENVOLIO

                    No, coz, I rather weep.

ROMEO

Good heart, at what?

BENVOLIO

                    At thy good heart's oppression.

ROMEO

Why, such is love's transgression.
Griefs of mine own lie heavy in my breast,
Which thou wilt propagate to have it pressed   185
With more of thine. This love that thou hast
   shown

27

188   *fume*   vapour.

189   *purged*   driven out, cleansed.

190   *vexed*   annoyed, upset.

191   *most discreet*   specific, particular.

192   *gall*   bitterness.

  preserving sweet   something fresh yet at the same time preserved or artificially kept fresh.

193   *Soft*   wait.

195–6   *Tut...other where*   Romeo admits that he's not behaving as he normally does because his mind is on other things (Rosaline).

197   *in sadness*   truthfully, but Romeo takes it up as a pun in the sense of being sad.

201   *ill urged*   unfortunately used.

203   *aimed so near*   guessed as much. Benvolio begins a hunting metaphor which is sustained over the next eight lines.

204   *mark-man*   marksman; Benvolio has guessed accurately.

205   *right fair mark*   clear target. Fair meaning beautiful is also suggested here.

Doth add more grief to too much of mine own.
Love is a smoke made with the fume of sighs:
Being purged, a fire sparkling in lovers' eyes;
Being vexed, a sea nourished with loving tears.   190
What is it else? A madness most discreet,
A choking gall, and a preserving sweet.
Farewell, my coz.

BENVOLIO

                Soft, I will go along;
And if you leave me so, you do me wrong.

ROMEO

Tut, I have lost myself; I am not here.   195
This is not Romeo; he's some other where.

BENVOLIO

Tell me in sadness, who is that you love?

ROMEO

What, shall I groan and tell thee?

BENVOLIO

                      Groan? Why no.
But sadly tell me who.

ROMEO

A sick man in sadness makes his will   200
A word ill urged to one that is so ill.
In sadness, cousin, I do love a woman.

BENVOLIO

I aimed so near when I supposed you loved.

ROMEO

A right good mark-man! And she's fair I love.

BENVOLIO

A right fair mark, fair coz, is soonest hit.   205

207 *with Cupid's arrow* see note to lines 169–70. If she were targeted by Cupid she would undoubtedly fall in love.

     she hath Dian's wit Diana, goddess of the hunt and chastity swore never to be married. Rosaline has done the same, and therefore thinks in the same way as Diana.

208 *proof* armour, protective clothing.

209 *childish* Cupid was the son of Venus, the goddess of love, and as such is usually depicted as a young boy.

210 *stay the seige* give in to.

211 *bide th' encounter...eyes* put up with loving gazes; 'assailing' means attacking: Romeo is continuing with the imagery of war begun on line 208.

212 *Nor ope...gold* nor let herself be won over with presents that would tempt even a saint.

214 *store* supply (of beauty).

215 *still live chaste* always remain a virgin.

216 *sparing* refusal to give in.

218 *Cuts beauty...posterity* she cannot pass her beauty on to others: the same idea as lines 213–14.

220 *merit bliss* be worthy to enter heaven.

221 *forsworn* promised she will not.

25–6 *By giving...beauties* look around you at other beautiful girls.

26–7 *'T is the way...more* doing that only makes one realise that she is more beautiful than all the others.

ROMEO

Well, in that hit you miss. She'll not be hit
With Cupid's arrow; she hath Dian's wit,
And in strong proof of chastity well-armed,
From Love's weak childish bow she lives un-
    charmed.
She will not stay the siege of loving terms,   210
Nor bide th' encounter of assailing eyes,
Nor ope her lap to saint-seducing gold.
O, she is rich in beauty; only poor
That when she dies, with beauty dies her store.

BENVOLIO

Then she hath sworn that she will still live chaste? 215

ROMEO

She hath, and in that sparing makes huge waste,
For beauty, starved with her severity,
Cuts beauty off from all posterity.
She is too fair, too wise, wisely too fair,
To merit bliss by making me despair.   220
She hath forsworn to love, and in that vow
Do I live dead, that live to tell it now.

BENVOLIO

Be ruled by me; forget to think of her.

ROMEO

O, teach me how I should forget to think!

BENVOLIO

By giving liberty unto thine eyes: 225
Examine other beauties.

ROMEO

                        'T is the way
To call hers – exquisite – in question more.

228 *happy masks*   small black masks were often worn by noble ladies when they ventured out in public; the masks are fortunate because they can touch what Romeo cannot (their faces).

232 *passing*   surpassing, fairer than all others.

233 *note*   reminder.

234 *passed*   surpassed.

236 *I'll pay...in debt*   I will teach you to forget if it kills me.

1–2 *bound...in penalty alike*   both are bound over to keep the peace or pay the same fine.

4 *reckoning*   reputation.

5 *at odds*   not agreeing with one another.

6 *suit*   request to marry Juliet.

7 *But saying o'er*   repeating.

9 *change*   passing of the seasons.

9–11 *She hath not seen...a bride*   fourteen was not thought to be too young for girls to marry in Mediterranean countries at the time; however Capulet still would like to delay the marriage until she is sixteen or so.

These happy masks that kiss fair ladies' brows.
Being black, puts us in mind they hide the fair.
He that is strucken blind cannot forget   230
The precious treasure of his eyesight lost.
Show me a mistress that is passing fair:
What doth her beauty serve, but as a note
Where I may read who passed that passing fair?
Farewell; thou canst not teach me to forget.   235

BENVOLIO
I'll pay that doctrine, or else die in debt.

Exeunt

Scene two

The same.

Enter CAPULET, PARIS *and the* CLOWN, *Capulet's servant.*

CAPULET
But Montague is bound as well as I,
In penalty alike, and 't is not hard, I think,
For men so old as we to keep the peace.

PARIS
Of honourable reckoning are you both,
And pity 't is you lived at odds so long.   5
But now, my lord, what say you to my suit?

CAPULET
But saying o'er what I have said before:
My child is yet a stranger in the world;
She hath not seen the change of fourteen years;
Let two more summers wither in their pride   10
Ere we may think her ripe to be a bride.

13 *marred*   spoiled (there was a very high incidence of young mothers dying in childbirth).

14 *Earth has swallowèd...she*   Capulet's other children (his hopes for the future) have all died young.

16 *get her heart*   win her love.

17 *My will...but a part*   you will need her agreement as well as my permission if you want to marry her.

18 *And*   if.

   within her scope of choice   depending on what she chooses.

19 *fair according*   agreeing.

20 *old accustomed*   long established.

21 *Whereto*   to which.

22 *the store*   them, the number.

24 *poor*   humble (he is being modest).

25 *Earth-treading stars*   young girls who are as bright and beautiful as the stars.

26 *lusty*   energetic.

27–8 *well-apparelled...treads*   well-dressed spring follows on the heels of tired worn-out winter. (The time of year when the sap begins to rise and a young man's thoughts are said to turn to the fairer sex.)

29 *fresh female buds*   adolescent girls.

30 *Inherit*   enjoy.

32–3 *Which one more...none*   you may notice Juliet among all these young beauties (again Capulet is being modest about his daughter's beauty).

34 *sirrah*   a way of speaking to servants.

   trudge about   walk around.

37 *stay*   wait.

38–44 *Find them out...the learned*   in these lines the Clown, who cannot read the guest list he has been given, says that men should stick to what they do best, and that this is not his strong point. He manages to get the proverbial tradesmen and their tools jumbled in the process.

PARIS

Younger than she are happy mothers made.

CAPULET

And too soon marred are those so early made.
Earth hath swallowèd all my hopes but she;
She's the hopeful lady of my earth.   15
But woo her, gentle Paris, get her heart;
My will to her consent is but a part.
And she agreed, within her scope of choice
Lies my consent and fair according voice.
This night I hold an old accustomed feast,   20
Whereto I have invited many a guest,
Such as I love; and you among the store,
One more most welcome, makes my number more.
At my poor house look to behold this night
Earth-treading stars that make dark heaven light.   25
Such comfort as do lusty young men feel
When well-apparelled April on the heel
Of limping winter treads, even such delight
Among fresh female buds shall you this night
Inherit at my house; hear all, all see,   30
And like her most whose merit most shall be:
Which one more view of many, mine being one,
May stand in number, though in reckoning none.
Come, go with me. (*To the* CLOWN, *giving him a paper*)
    Go, sirrah, trudge about
Through fair Verona; find those persons out   35
Whose names are written there, and to them say
My house and welcome on their pleasure stay.

Exeunt CAPULET *and* PARIS

CLOWN

Find them out whose names are written here? It is

35

40 *last* shoemaker's wooden template.

44 *I must to the learned* I must find someone who can read.

45 *In good time* just in time.

47 *One pain...anguish* any pain hurts less if another one begins in another part of the body.

48 *Turn giddy...turning* if you get dizzy it helps to turn in the opposite direction.

49 *cures with* is cured by.

languish suffering (caused by another worry).

50–1 *Take thou...old will die* love was supposedly an infection caught through the eyes, so by looking at other girls the poison of being in love with Rosaline will' go away.

52 *plantain leaf* this leaf was supposed to help soothe cuts. Romeo is teasing Benvolio by taking his advice literally.

53 *broken* cut, damaged. (Romeo has probably just delivered a kick to Benvolio's shin!)

55 *bound* confined, chained (lunatics were treated little better than animals in Shakespeare's time).

57 *e'en* evening, but used after midday.

58 *God gi'* God give you.

written that the shoemaker should meddle with his
yard and the tailor with his last, the fisher with his   40
pencil and the painter with his nets. But I am sent
to find those persons whose names are here writ,
and can never find what names the writing person
hath here writ. I must to the learned. (*He sees*
BENVOLIO *and* ROMEO *approaching*) In good time!   45

Enter BENVOLIO *and* ROMEO.

BENVOLIO
Tut, man, one fire burns out another's burning,
One pain is lessened by another's anguish;
Turn giddy, and be holp by backward turning.
One desperate grief cures with another's languish:
Take thou some new infection to thy eye,   50
And the rank poison of the old will die.

ROMEO
Your plantain leaf is excellent for that.

BENVOLIO
For what, I pray thee?

ROMEO
                    For your broken shin.

BENVOLIO
Why, Romeo, art thou mad?

ROMEO
Not mad, but bound more than a madman is;   55
Shut up in prison, kept without my food,
Whipped and tormented, and – Good e'en, good
   fellow.

CLOWN
God gi' good e'en. I pray, sir, can you read?

59 *Ay...misery* yes, I can tell ('read') what my luck is like by seeing how sad I am.

63 *rest you merry* goodbye.

66 *County* Count.

74 *Whither* where.

ROMEO

Ay, mine own fortune in my misery.

CLOWN

Perhaps you have learned it without book. But I 60
pray, can you read anything you see?

ROMEO

Ay, if I know the letters and the language.

CLOWN

Ye say honestly; rest you merry. (*He moves off*)

ROMEO

Stay, fellow; I can read. (*He reads the list*)
"Signor Martino and his wife and daughters; 65
County Anselme and his beauteous sisters;
The lady widow of Vitruvio;
Signor Placentio and his lovely nieces;
Mercutio and his brother Valentine;
Mine uncle Capulet, his wife and daughters, 70
My fair niece Rosaline and Livia;
Signor Valentio and his cousin Tybalt;
Lucio and the lively Helena".
A fair assembly. Whither should they come?

CLOWN

Up – 75

ROMEO

Whither? To supper?

CLOWN

To our house.

ROMEO

Whose house?

83 *crush*   drink (this comes from crushing the grapes to make wine).

88 *unattainted*   unbiased.

90 *I will make...a crow*   I will show you that she is not as beautiful as others (swans are white and graceful, crows dark and ugly).

91 *religion*   in this case, love. (The metaphor of love as a religion is sustained over the next five lines.)

92 *Maintains such falsehood*   believes such lies.

93 *And these*   Romeo's eyes.

94 *heretics*   those who did not hold expected religious beliefs were often drowned, or burned at the stake.

96 *match*   like, one to match her.

97 *you saw...else being by*   you saw her as beautiful because no other girls were nearby to compare her with.

98 *poised with*   balanced with. Romeo cannot take his eyes from Rosaline and her image is in both of his eyes, which Benvolio likens to a pair of scales. If he were to take one eye from her to look at another girl then the latter's beauty might outweigh Rosaline's in the balance.

102 *scant*   hardly.

CLOWN

My master's.

ROMEO

Indeed, I should have asked thee that before.   80

CLOWN

Now I'll tell you without asking. My master is the
great rich Capulet; and if you be not of the house of
Montagues, I pray come and crush a cup of wine.
Rest you merry.

Exit CLOWN

BENVOLIO

At this same ancient feast of Capulet's   85
Sups the fair Rosaline whom thou so loves,
With all the admirèd beauties of Verona.
Go thither, and with unattainted eye,
Compare her face with some that I shall show,
And I will make thee think thy swan a crow.   90

ROMEO

When the devout religion of mine eye
Maintains such falsehood, then turn tears to fire;
And these, who, often drowned, could never die,
Transparent heretics, be burnt for liars.
One fairer than my love? The all-seeing sun   95
Ne'er saw her match since first the world begun.

BENVOLIO

Tut, you saw her fair, none else being by,
Herself poised with herself in either eye;
But in that crystal scales let there be weighed
Your lady's love against some other maid   100
That I will show you shining at this feast,
And she shall scant show well that now seems best.

104 *mine own* my own loved one, or Rosaline.

2 *maidenhead* virginity (probably lost at twelve!).
3 *What* exclamation, rather than a question.
7 *What is your will?* polite way of asking what do you want.
8 *the matter* what I want to talk about.
  give leave leave us alone.
10 *thou's* you must.
11 *pretty* suitable (for marriage).

ROMEO
I'll go along, no such sight to be shown,
But to rejoice in splendour of mine own.

Exeunt

Scene three

A room in Capulet's house.

Enter LADY CAPULET *and* NURSE.

LADY CAPULET
Nurse, where's my daughter? Call her forth to me.

NURSE
Now, by my maidenhead at twelve year old, I bade
her come. What, lamb! What, lady-bird! God forbid! Where's this girl? What, Juliet!

Enter JULIET.

JULIET
How now? Who calls? 5

NURSE
Your mother.

JULIET
Madam, I am here. What is your will?

LADY CAPULET
This is the matter. Nurse, give leave a while;
We must talk in secret. (NURSE *begins to leáve*) Nurse,
come back again;
I have remembered me, thou's hear our counsel. 10
Thou know'st my daughter's of a pretty age.

14 *teen*   sadness.

16 *Lammas-tide*   1 August.

17 *odd*   a few.

20 *of an age*   the same age.

21 *Susan is with God*   the Nurse's own daughter, Susan, is dead. She was born at the same time as Juliet and so the Nurse would have been employed to wet-nurse (breast-feed) Juliet alongside her own child. Lady Capulet may have been unable to give milk or just considered it unladylike.

23 *marry*   by the Virgin Mary, a mild swear word.

26–7 *laid wormwood to my dug*   placed the juice of a bitter plant on her nipple to discourage the child from sucking and to wean her on to solid food.

29 *I do bear a brain*   I have a good memory.

31 *tetchy*   bad-tempered.

32 *'Shake', quoth the dove-house*   the dovecote moves because of the earthquake.

33 *I trow*   believe me.

   bid me trudge   tell me to get out of the way.

35 *high-lone*   by herself.

   by the rood   by the cross (on which Christ was crucified), an oath.

37 *broke her brow*   cut her forehead.

NURSE

Faith, I can tell her age unto an hour.

LADY CAPULET

She's not fourteen.

NURSE

I'll lay fourteen of my teeth – and yet, to my teen be
it spoken, I have but four – she's not fourteen. How 15
long is it now to Lammas-tide?

LADY CAPULET

A fortnight and odd days.

NURSE

Even or odd, of all days in the year come Lammas-
Eve at night shall she be fourteen. Susan and she –
God rest all Christian souls – were of an age. Well, 20
Susan is with God; she was too good for me. But, as
I said, on Lammas-Eve at night shall she be fourteen; that shall she, marry; I remember it well. 'T is
since the earthquake now eleven years, and she was
weaned – I never shall forget it – of all the days of 25
the year, upon that day; for I had then laid wormwood to my dug, sitting in the sun under the dove-
house wall. My lord and you were then at Mantua –
nay, I do bear a brain! But, as I said, when it did
taste the wormwood on the nipple of my dug and 30
felt it bitter, pretty fool, to see it tetchy, and fall out
with the dug! "Shake", quoth the dove-house.
'Twas no need, I trow, to bid me trudge. And since
that time it is eleven years for then she could stand
high-lone; nay, by the rood, she could have run and 35
waddled all about, for even the day before, she
broke her brow, and then my husband – God be

38 *'a*   he.

40–1 *Thou wilt...Jule?*   when you know more about things you will fall on to your back. He is being cheerfully vulgar and the Nurse obviously enjoys this kind of humour, suggesting that they were well-matched.

41 *holidame*   holy dame, referring to the Virgin Mary – a mild swear word.

43–4 *I warrant, and I should*   I'll wager that even if I should.

46 *it stinted*   she stopped crying. Nurse often refers to the infant Juliet as 'it' here.

47 *hold thy peace*   keep quiet.

51 *stone*   testicle.

   perilous   dangerous.

57 *mark thee to his grace*   save your soul.

59 *once*   one day.

63 *How stands...married?*   how do you feel about the idea of getting married?

with his soul, 'a was a merry man – took up the
child. "Yea," quoth he, "dost thou fall upon thy
face? Thou wilt fall backward when thou hast more 40
wit, wilt thou not, Jule?" And, by my holidame, the
pretty wretch left crying, and said "Ay". To see
now how a jest shall come about! I warrant, and I
should live a thousand years, I never should forget
it. "Wilt thou not, Jule?" quoth he; and, pretty fool, 45
it stinted, and said "Ay".

LADY CAPULET
Enough of this. I pray thee hold thy peace.

NURSE
Yes, madam; yet I cannot choose but laugh, to
think it should leave crying, and say "Ay"; and yet
I warrant it had upon it brow a bump as big as a 50
young cockerel's stone – a perilous knock – and it
cried bitterly. "Yea," quoth my husband, "fall'st
upon thy face? Thou wilt fall backward when thou
comest to age, wilt thou not, Jule? It stinted, and
said "Ay".   55

JULIET
And stint thou too, I pray thee, Nurse, say I.

NURSE
Peace, I have done. God mark thee to his grace,
thou wast the prettiest babe that e'er I nursed. And
I might live to see thee married once, I have my
wish.   60

LADY CAPULET
Marry, that "marry" is the very theme
I came to talk of. Tell me, daughter Juliet,
How stands your dispositions to be married?

66 *from thy teat* with your milk; in other words she has learnt this from the Nurse herself.

69 *count* calculations.

70 *upon these years* at your age.

74 *a man of wax* ideal man (a model).

81 *every married lineament* every one of his perfect features.

82 *one...content* they complement one another.

84 *margent* margin.

86 *a cover* Lady Capulet has compared Paris to a book which only needs a cover to complete it; in other words a wife to enfold him in her arms.

JULIET

It is an honour that I dream not of.

NURSE

An honour! Were not I thine only nurse, I would   65
say thou hadst sucked wisdom from thy teat.

LADY CAPULET

Well, think of marriage now. Younger than you,
Here in Verona, ladies of esteem,
Are made already mothers. By my count,
I was your mother much upon these years   70
That you are now a maid. Thus then in brief,
The valiant Paris seeks you for his love.

NURSE

A man, young lady! Lady, such a man as all the
world . . . why, he's a man of wax!

LADY CAPULET

Verona's summer hath not such a flower.   75

NURSE

Nay, he's a flower; in faith, a very flower.

LADY CAPULET

What say you? Can you love the gentleman?
This night you shall behold him at our feast.
Read o'er the volume of young Paris' face,
And find delight writ there with beauty's pen; 80
Examine every married lineament,
And see how one another lends content;
And what obscured in this fair volume lies,
Find written in the margent of his eyes.
This precious book of love, this unbound lover, 85
To beautify him, only lacks a cover.

88 *For fair without...to hide*   an attractive cover will hide a good book within it.

89–90 *That book...story*   Juliet's social standing will increase if she marries Paris.

93 *Women grow by men*   get pregnant – the Nurse has missed the point of Lady Capulet's speech.

95 *I'll look...move*   I'll look on him kindly and perhaps will like him.

96 *endart*   pierce.

97 *Than your consent...fly*   but I need your permission to let myself fall in love.

100 *in extremity*   needs to be sorted out urgently.

   I must hence   I must go from here.

101 *wait*   serve.

   straight   immediately.

102 *stays*   is waiting.

103 *to*   and.

The fish lives in the sea; and 't is much pride
For fair without, the fair within to hide.
That book in many's eyes doth share the glory
That in gold clasps locks in the golden story: 90
So shall you share all that he doth possess
By having him, making yourself no less.

NURSE

No less? Nay, bigger! Women grow by men.

LADY CAPULET

Speak briefly: can you like of Paris' love?

JULIET

I'll look to like, if looking liking move;   95
But no more deep will I endart mine eye
Than your consent gives strength to make it fly.

Enter CLOWN.

CLOWN

Madam, the guests are come, supper served up, you
called, my young lady asked for, the Nurse cursed in
the pantry, and everything in extremity. I must 100
hence to wait. I beseech you, follow straight.

LADY CAPULET

We follow thee. Juliet, the County stays.

NURSE

Go, girl; seek happy nights to happy days.

Exeunt

51

masked   masked balls were very popular in Shakespeare's time (see also *Much Ado About Nothing*) and the Montagues can easily go to this one in their enemy's own house without fear of being recognised.

1   *spoke for our excuse*   they have a speech ready if their identities should be discovered.

2   *shall we on without apology*   shall we go on in without explaining our presence?

3   *The date...prolixity*   it's old-fashioned to make complicated excuses.

4   *no Cupid hoodwinked*   no blindfolded Cupid (see note to Act 1, scene 1, lines 169–70).

5   *Tartar's painted bow of lath*   shaped in the same way as Cupid's bow of thin wood.

6   *crow-keeper*   scarecrow.

7   *without-book*   ad-libbed.

8   *After the prompter*   following the prompter (who whispers lines to actors when they forget them).

9   *measure*   assess, judge.

10   *We'll...measure*   we'll dance (a measure) with them.

11   *ambling*   dancing (those holding torches obviously would not dance).

12   *heavy*   melancholy.

16   *stakes*   bear-baiting was a popular entertainment in Shakespeare's day, the bear being tied to a stake.

18   *bound*   leap.

Scene four

Outside Capulet's house.

Enter torchbearers, followed by ROMEO, MERCUTIO, BENVOLIO
and five or six other masked men.

ROMEO

    What, shall this speech be spoke for our excuse,
    Or shall we on without apology?

BENVOLIO

    The date is out of such prolixity:
    We'll have no Cupid hoodwinked with a scarf,
    Bearing a Tartar's painted bow of lath,   5
    Scaring the ladies like a crow-keeper;
    Nor no without-book prologue, faintly spoke
    After the prompter, for our entrance.
    But let them measure us by what they will,
    We'll measure them a measure and be gone.   10

ROMEO

    Give me a torch: I am not for this ambling;
    Being but heavy, I will bear the light.

MERCUTIO

    Nay, gentle Romeo, we must have you dance.

ROMEO

    Not I, believe me. You have dancing shoes
    With nimble soles: I have a soul of lead   15
    So stakes me to the ground I cannot move.

MERCUTIO

    You are a lover: borrow Cupid's wings,
    And soar with them above a common bound.

19 *sore empiercèd*   sorely wounded.

20 *bound*   tied up.

21 *bound a pitch*   leap to the height to which a falcon soars. Note the continued play on the word 'bound'.

26 *rude*   coarse.

28 *Prick love for pricking*   if love is hurting you hurt it in return: Mercutio also suggests that men must overpower women in love-making.

29 *case*   mask.

visage   face.

30 *A visor for a visor*   a mask to suit the face (i.e. ugly).

31 *curious*   inquisitive.

quote deformities   take note of ugliness.

32 *beetle brows...for me*   Mercutio describes his mask; it has bushy eyebrows and is probably red in colour.

34 *betake him to his legs*   join in the dancing.

35 *wantons*   revellers.

36 *the senseless rushes*   rushes or reeds were strewn on the floors of buildings to act as a scented covering instead of carpet and were later swept away with the debris. Romeo is being scornful about dancers and he transfers the epithet 'senseless' from them to the rushes that will be trodden under their feet.

37 *proverbed with a grandsire phrase*   backed up by an old-fashioned saying.

40 *dun*   grey and therefore inconspicuous (Mercutio is punning with the word 'done' in the previous line).

41 *If thou...the mire*   Mercutio teases Romeo for being a sullen stick-in-the-mud. Horses were often given the name Dun, and as they could get stuck in mud (or 'mire') and had to be pulled out, so Mercutio is determined that Romeo can be hauled out of his sad mood.

ROMEO

I am too sore empiercèd with his shaft
To soar with his light feathers; and so bound,   20
I cannot bound a pitch above dull woe.
Under love's heavy burden do I sink.

MERCUTIO

And to sink in it should you burden love –
Too great oppression for a tender thing.

ROMEO

Is love a tender thing? It is too rough,   25
Too rude, too boisterous, and it pricks like thorn.

MERCUTIO

If love be rough with you, be rough with love:
Prick love for pricking, and you beat love down.
Give me a case to put my visage in:
A visor for a visor! What care I   30
What curious eye doth quote deformities?
Here are the beetle brows shall blush for me.

He puts on a mask.

BENVOLIO

Come, knock and enter; and no sooner in,
But every man betake him to his legs.

ROMEO

A torch for me: let wantons light of heart   35
Tickle the senseless rushes with their heels,
For I am proverbed with a grandsire phrase:
I'll be a candle-holder and look on.
The game was ne'er so fair, and I am done.

MERCUTIO

Tut, dun's the mouse, the constable's own word;   40
If thou art Dun, we'll draw thee from the mire,

42 *save your reverence*   begging your pardon, sir.

43 *burn daylight*   waste time.

45–6 *Take our good meaning...five wits*   don't take everything I say too seriously, just grasp the general gist.

49 *'t is no wit*   it is not sensible.

50 *tonight*   last night.

53 *Queen Mab*   queen of the fairies in Celtic myth.

Or, save your reverence, love, wherein thou stickest
Up to the ears. Come, we burn daylight, ho.

ROMEO

Nay, that's not so.

MERCUTIO

I mean, sir, in delay
We waste our lights in vains, like lights by day. 45
Take our good meaning, for our judgement sits
Five times in that, ere once in our five wits.

ROMEO

And we mean well in going to this masque,
But 't is no wit to go.

MERCUTIO

Why, may one ask?

ROMEO

I dreamt a dream tonight.

MERCUTIO

And so did I. 50

ROMEO

Well, what was yours?

MERCUTIO

That dreamers often lie.

ROMEO

In bed asleep while they do dream things true.

MERCUTIO

O then I see Queen Mab hath been with you.

BENVOLIO

Queen Mab? What's she?

55 *midwife* she brings forth dreams and fantasies.

56 *agate* semi-precious stone, small because they were used in signet rings.

57 *alderman* town councillor.

58 *atomies* very small creatures.

59 *Athwart* astride.

60 *spinners'* spiders'.

62 *traces* reins.

64 *film* gossamer, spider's web.

67 *the lazy finger of a maid* worms were supposed to breed from the fingers of idle people.

69 *joiner-squirrel* the squirrel is like a carpenter in the way he hollows out nuts.

70 *Time out o' mind* for as long as anyone can remember.

73 *curtsies* bowing and similar flattery (which could help them win favour in court).

79 *smelling out a suit* finding someone who will pay him handsomely for mentioning their name at court.

80 *tithe-pig* parsons received tithes (a tenth of a parishioner's earnings) towards their upkeep and that of their church. This was not always paid in money but could be in goods or livestock, as the pig is here.

82 *benefice* church income.

85 *breaches* breaking through walls.

ambuscadoes ambushes.

Spanish blades swords of particularly fine quality came from Toledo in Spain.

MERCUTIO
<pre>
She is the fairies' midwife, and she comes   55
In shape no bigger than an agate stone
On the forefinger of an alderman,
Drawn with a team of little atomies
Athwart men's noses as they lie asleep.
Her waggon spokes made of long spinners' legs,   60
The cover of the wings of grasshoppers,
Her traces of the smallest spider-web,
Her collars of the moonshine's watery beams,
Her whip of cricket's bone, the lash of film,
Her waggoner a small grey-coated gnat,   65
Not half so big as a round little worm
Pricked from the lazy finger of a maid.
Her chariot is an empty hazel-nut,
Made by the joiner-squirrel or old grub,
Time out o' mind the fairies' coachmakers.   70
And in this state she gallops night by night
Through lovers' brains, and then they dream of
     love;
O'er courtiers' knees, that dream on curtsies
     straight;
O'er lawyers' fingers, who straight dream on fees;
O'er ladies' lips, who straight on kisses dream,   75
Which oft the angry Mab with blisters plagues,
Because their breaths with sweetmeats tainted are.
Sometime she gallops o'er a courtier's nose
And then dreams he of smelling out a suit;
And sometime comes she with a tithe-pig's tail,   80
Tickling a parson's nose as 'a lies asleep,
And then dreams he of another benefice;
Sometime she driveth o'er a soldier's neck,
And then dreams he of cutting foreign throats,
Of breaches, ambuscadoes, Spanish blades,   85
</pre>

86 *healths five fathom deep*   drinking heavily.

   anon   straight away.

91 *bakes the elf-locks in foul sluttish hairs*   tangles the hair of those who do not take care of themselves.

93 *hag*   evil spirit.

94 *learns them first to bear*   teaches them how: i) to take the weight of their lovers ii) to give birth to children.

95 *carriage*   this also has a double meaning: i) child-bearing ii) deportment or grace.

95 *Begot of...fantasy*   born of no more than idle dreaming.

101 *inconstant*   unreliable, like the wind which keeps changing direction.

105 *blows us from ourselves*   makes us forget what we are meant to be doing.

107–8 *my mind misgives...in the stars*   I have a fear at the back of my mind of some unfortunate incident which has not yet been revealed.

Of healths five fathom deep, and then anon
Drums in his ear, at which he starts and wakes,
And being thus frighted, swears a prayer or two,
And sleeps again. This is that very Mab
That plaits the manes of horses in the night,   90
And bakes the elf-locks in foul sluttish hairs,
Which once untangled, much misfortune bodes;
This is the hag, when maids lie on their backs,
That presses them and learns them first to bear,
Making them women of good carriage;   95
This is she –

ROMEO

    Peace, peace, Mercutio, peace!
Thou talk'st of nothing.

MERCUTIO

     True, I talk of dreams,
Which are the children of an idle brain,
Begot of nothing but vain fantasy,
Which is as thin of substance as the air,   100
And more inconstant than the wind, who woos
Even now the frozen bosom of the north,
And being angered, puffs away from thence,
Turning his face to the dew-dropping south.

BENVOLIO

This wind you talk of blows us from ourselves: 105
Supper is done, and we shall come too late.

ROMEO

I fear, too early, for my mind misgives
Some consequence, yet hanging in the stars,
Shall bitterly begin his fearful date
With this night's revels, and expire the term   110

112 *some vile...death* life that will be lost before its time.
113 *He that hath...of my course* God who guides my life.

1 *take* clear.
2 *trencher* wooden plate.
5 *court-cupboard* sideboard.
6 *look to the plate* look after the silver.
7 *march-pane* marzipan.

Of a despisèd life closed in my breast,
By some vile forfeit of untimely death:
But He that hath the steerage of my course
Direct my sail. On, lusty gentlemen.

BENVOLIO
Strike, drum.   115

Exeunt

Scene five

The hall in Capulet's house.

Enter ROMEO *and the other* MASKERS *and stand at one side of the stage. Enter two* SERVANTS.

FIRST SERVANT
Where's Potpan, that he helps not to take away? He shift a trencher? He scrape a trencher?

SECOND SERVANT
When good manners shall lie all in one or two men's hands, and they unwashed too, 'tis a foul thing.

FIRST SERVANT
Away with the joint-stools, remove the court-   5
cupboard, look to the plate. Good thou, save me a piece of march-pane, and, as thou loves me, let the porter let in Susan Grindstone and Nell. (*He calls*) Antony and Potpan!

Enter the servants, ANTONY *and* POTPAN.

ANTONY
Ay, boy, ready.   10

13 *Cheerly* cheer up.

3–14 *be brisk...take all* probably part of an old proverb that seems to suggest that one might as well enjoy oneself as Death is inevitable.

16 *walk a bout* dance.

18 *makes dainty* either dances on her toes, or refuses to dance.

19 *Am I come near ye now?* have I hit the nail on the head? Have I guessed the truth?

25 *foot it* dance.

26 *turn the tables up* trestle tables would probably be taken apart and moved away after the feast to make room for the dancing.

28 *unlooked-for* unexpected.

FIRST SERVANT

You are looked for and called for, asked for and
sought for, in the great chamber.

POTPAN

We cannot be here, and there too. Cheerly, boys; be
brisk a while, and the longer liver take all.

Exeunt SERVANTS

Enter LORD *and* LADY CAPULET, JULIET, TYBALT, NURSE,
the GUESTS *and* MUSICIANS *at one side of the stage, meeting the*
MASKERS *who are at the other side.*

CAPULET

Welcome, gentlemen. Ladies that have their toes   15
Unplagued with corns will walk a bout with you.
Ah ha, my mistresses! which of you all
Will now deny to dance? She that makes dainty,
She, I'll swear, hath corns. Am I come near ye
    now?
Welcome, gentlemen. I have seen the day   20
That I have worn a visor, and could tell
A whispering tale in a fair lady's ear
Such as would please; 't is gone, 't is gone, 't is
    gone.
You are welcome, gentlemen. Come, musicians,
    play!

Music plays and they dance.

A hall, a hall! Give room, and foot it, girls.   25
(*To the* SERVANTS) More light you knaves, and
    turn the tables up,
And quench the fire, the room is grown too hot.
(*To himself*) Ah, sirrah, this unlooked-for sport
    comes well.

32 *By'r Lady*   by the Virgin Mary.

34 *nuptial*   wedding.

35 *Come Pentecost...will*   when Whit-Sunday comes around in its own good time.

39 *but a ward*   still a minor (under twenty-one).

46 *Ethiop*   literally Ethiopian but used for anyone of African descent.

47 *Beauty...too dear*   too valuable to be seen and made use of on this earth.

(*To his cousin*) Nay sit, nay sit, good cousin Capulet,
For you and I are past our dancing days.   30
How long is 't now since last yourself and I
Were in a mask?

COUSIN
            By 'r Lady, thirty years.

CAPULET
   What, man? 'T is not so much, 't is not so much:
'T is since the nuptial of Lucentio –
Come Pentecost as quickly as it will –   35
Some five and twenty years, and then we masked.

COUSIN
   'T is more, 't is more; his son is elder, sir:
His son is thirty.

CAPULET
            Will you tell me that?
His son was but a ward two years ago.
(*Observing the dancers*) Good youths i' faith. O
   youth's a jolly thing.   40

ROMEO
   (*To a servant*) What lady's that which doth enrich
the hand of yonder knight?

SERVANT
   I know not, sir.

ROMEO
   (*To himself*) O she doth teach the torches to burn
   bright!
It seems she hangs upon the cheek of night   45
As a rich jewel in an Ethiop's ear;
Beauty too rich for use, for earth too dear.

48 *So shows...with crows*   a white dove looks like this among crows. (Think back to Benvolio's words in Act 1, scene 2, line 90.)

49 *fellows*   friends.

50 *The measure...of stand*   I'll watch where she stands when the dance is over.

52 *Forswear*   deny.

55 *rapier*   fencing sword.

    slave   by calling him a servant, Tybalt suggests that Romeo is his inferior.

56 *antic face*   hideous mask.

57 *fleer*   mock.

    solemnity   celebration.

58 *by the stock and honour of my kin*   by the honour of my family name and ancestry.

60 *Wherefore storm you so?*   why are you shouting and blustering like this?

65 *Content thee*   calm down.

66 *portly*   dignified.

68 *well-governed*   sensible.

70 *do him disparagement*   slight him, speak badly of him.

So shows a snowy dove trooping with crows,
As yonder lady o'er her fellows shows.
The measure done, I'll watch her place of stand,   50
And, touching hers, make blessèd my rude hand.
Did my heart love till now? Forswear it, sight,
For I ne'er saw true beauty till this night.

TYBALT
This, by his voice, should be a Montague.
Fetch me my rapier, boy. (*Exit page*) What dares the
    slave   55
Come hither, covered with an antic face,
To fleer and scorn at our solemnity?
Now, by the stock and honour of my kin,
To strike him dead, I hold it not a sin.

CAPULET
Why, how now, kinsman! Wherefore storm you so? 60

TYBALT
Uncle, this is a Montague, our foe;
A villain that is hither come in spite,
To scorn at our solemnity this night.

CAPULET
Young Romeo is it?

TYBALT
                    'T is he, that villain, Romeo.

CAPULET
Content thee, gentle coz, let him alone;   65
'A bears him like a portly gentleman:
And to say truth, Verona brags of him
To be a virtuous and well-governed youth.
I would not, for the wealth of all this town,
Here in my house do him disparagement;   70

73 *Show a fair presence*   look as if you are in a good mood.

74 *ill-beseeming semblance*   unfitting look.

77 *goodman boy*   Capulet is being sarcastic to Tybalt who refuses to do as he is
  asked.

  Go to!   stop it!

79 *God shall mend my soul*   as God shall save me.

80 *mutiny*   riot.

81 *set cock-a-hoop*   cause a fuss.

  You'll be the man!   you have to pretend to be a big man and throw your weight
  around.

83 *saucy*   insolent, cheeky.

84 *This trick...you*   you will get yourself into trouble.

85 *contrary*   go against.

86 *princox*   rude youth.

89 *Patience...meeting*   patience, when forced to overule my strong anger.

Therefore be patient, take no note of him.
It is my will, the which if thou respect,
Show a fair presence and put off these frowns,
An ill-beseeming semblance for a feast.

TYBALT
It fits when such a villain is a guest.   75
I'll not endure him.

CAPULET
                        He shall be endured.
What, goodman boy? I say he shall. Go to!
Am I the master here, or you? Go to!
You'll not endure him! God shall mend my soul,
You'll make a mutiny among my guests!   80
You will set cock-a-hoop! You'll be the man!

TYBALT
Why, uncle, 't is a shame.

CAPULET
                        Go to, go to!
You are a saucy boy. Is 't so indeed?
This trick may chance to scathe you, I know what.
You must contrary me! Marry, 't is time –   85
(*To the dancers*) Well said, my hearts! (*To* TYBALT)
    You are a princox; go
Be quiet, or – (*To the* SERVANTS) More light, more
    light, for shame! –
(*To* TYBALT) I'll make you quiet. – (*To the dancers*)
    What, cheerly, my hearts!

He leaves TYBALT *and moves among the guests.*

TYBALT
    (*To himself*) Patience perforce with wilful choler
        meeting,

71

90 *different greeting*   clash of opposing feelings.

92 *gall*   poison.

93 *profane*   defile, sully.

94 *This holy shrine*   this sacred temple – meaning Juliet's hand.

98 *mannerly*   proper, well-mannered.

99 *saints*   statues of the saints.

100 *palmers'*   pilgrims to Jerusalem carried palm branches; Juliet is punning on this and the palm of the hand.

102 *Ay, pilgrim...in prayer*   Juliet is not prepared to grant the kiss immediately.

105 *Saints do not...sake*   statues of saints cannot move and yet they allow pilgrims to kiss them.

106 *my prayer's effect*   my kiss.

107 *purged*   washed away.

Makes my flesh tremble in their different greeting. 90
I will withdraw, but this intrusion shall,
Now seeming sweet, convert to bitterest gall.

Exit

ROMEO

(*Taking* JULIET's *hand*) If I profane with my un-
  worthiest hand
This holy shrine, the gentle sin is this:
My lips, two blushing pilgrims, ready stand 95
To smooth that rough touch with a tender kiss.

JULIET

Good pilgrim, you do wrong your hand too much,
Which mannerly devotion shows in this;
For saints have hands that pilgrims' hands do
  touch,
And palm to palm is holy palmers' kiss. 100

ROMEO

Have not saints lips, and holy palmers too?

JULIET

Ay, pilgrim, lips that they must use in prayer.

ROMEO

O then, dear saint, let lips do what hands do:
They pray, "Grant thou, lest faith turn to despair."

JULIET

Saints do not move, though grant for prayers' sake. 105

ROMEO

Then move not, while my prayer's effect I take.
Thus from my lips, by thine, my sin is purged.

He kisses her.

109 *O trespass sweetly urged!*   you encouraged this sin very sweetly.

110 *You kiss by the book*   like someone who has read, and therefore knows a lot about the subject.

117 *Shall have the chinks*   will have plenty of money (because she is the only child of rich Capulet).

118 *O dear account!*   what a high price to pay.

119 *The sport is at the best*   the best part of the night is over (presumably Benvolio realises that they have been discovered).

120 *the more is my unrest*   I feel more and more uneasy.

JULIET

Then have my lips the sin that they have took.

ROMEO

Sin from my lips? O trespass sweetly urged!
Give me my sin again.

He kisses her again.

JULIET

You kiss by the book.   110

NURSE *comes to* JULIET *from the side of the stage.*

NURSE

Madam, your mother craves a word with you.

JULIET *joins her mother at the side of the stage.*

ROMEO

What is her mother?

NURSE

Marry, bachelor,
Her mother is the lady of the house,
And a good lady, and a wise and virtuous.
I nursed her daughter that you talked withal.   115
I tell you, he that can lay hold of her
Shall have the chinks.

ROMEO

Is she a Capulet?
O dear account! My life is my foe's debt.

BENVOLIO

Away, be gone! The sport is at the best.

ROMEO

Ay, so I fear; the more is my unrest.   120

122 *a trifling foolish banquet towards*   we have a light supper laid on.
126 *by my fay*   by my faith.
     waxes   grows.
128 *yond gentleman*   that gentleman over there.
135 *My grave...bed*   I will die unmarried.

CAPULET

Nay, gentleman, prepare not to be gone:
We have a trifling foolish banquet towards.

The MASKERS *whisper their excuses to him.*

Is it e'en so? Why, then I thank you all.
I thank you, honest gentlemen; good night.
(*To the servants*) More torches here! Come on, then
    let's to bed.   125

> *Torchbearers show the maskers out*

(*To himself*) Ah, sirrah, by my fay, it waxes late.
I'll to my rest.

> *Exeunt all except* JULIET *and* NURSE

JULIET

Come hither, Nurse. What is yond gentleman?

NURSE

The son and heir of old Tiberio.

JULIET

What's he that now is going out of door?   130

NURSE

Marry, that I think be young Petruchio.

JULIET

What's he that follows there, that would not dance?

NURSE

I know not.

JULIET

Go ask his name (*Exit* NURSE) If he be marrièd,
My grave is like to be my wedding bed.   135

139 *Too early...too late!*   if I'd only realised who he was before I'd fallen in love with
     him.
140 *Prodigious*   ominous.
143 *Anon*   immediately.

NURSE

(*Returning*) His name is Romeo, and a Montague,
The only son of your great enemy.

JULIET

(*To herself*) My only love sprung from my only hate!
Too early seen unknown, and known too late!
Prodigious birth of love it is to me,   140
That I must love a loathèd enemy.

NURSE

What's this, what's this?

JULIET

                A rhyme I learnt even now
Of one I danced withal.

JULIET'S *mother calls her from another room.*

NURSE

                Anon, anon!
Come let's away; the strangers all are gone.

                                Exeunt

A film still from Franco Zeffirelli's production of **Romeo and Juliet, 1968.**

Act 2: summary

It is late on Sunday night, the day after the ball, and Romeo has slipped away from his friends into the orchard of Capulet's house. There he overhears Juliet, who is on her balcony, pledging her love for him. They exchange vows and she promises to send a messenger to him in the morning.

Early on Monday morning Romeo visits Friar Lawrence, who is gathering herbs for medicines and other potions. He asks the Friar to marry them in secret and, although Lawrence warns him about being too hasty, he finally agrees.

Meanwhile Benvolio and Mercutio wait, knowing that Romeo has received a letter from Tybalt challenging him to a duel. When Romeo arrives they are pleasantly surprised by his good spirits and they joke with him until Juliet's nurse appears. She receives Romeo's instructions and sets off to tell Juliet.

Juliet manages to leave the house that afternoon as she already has permission from her parents to go to confession. She meets Romeo at the Friar's cell and they are married there.

1 *old Desire*   Romeo's love for Rosaline.

2 *young Affection*   his love for Juliet.

gapes   longs.

3 *That fair*   Rosaline.

4 *matched*   compared.

5 *again*   in return.

6 *Alike*   both of them.

7 *foe-supposed*   as she is a Capulet, Juliet is supposed to be his enemy.

complain   express his love.

8 *fearful*   dangerous.

9 *held*   seen as.

10 *use to*   usually.

11 *means*   chances, opportunities.

14 *Tempering extremities*   softening the hardship.

1 *forward*   away from Juliet's house.

2 *dull earth*   his body is nothing but dull earth without Juliet.

centre   core; Juliet has become the centre of his world.

Act Two

Enter CHORUS.

CHORUS
    Now old Desire doth in his death-bed lie,
      And young Affection gapes to be his heir;
    That fair for which love groaned for and would die,
      With tender Juliet matched, is now not fair.
    Now Romeo is beloved and loves again,   5
      Alike bewitchèd by the charm of looks,
    But to his foe-supposed he must complain,
      And she steal love's sweet bait from fearful hooks:
    Being held a foe, he may not have access
      To breathe such vows as lovers use to swear;   10
    And she as much in love, her means much less
      To meet her new-belovèd anywhere;
    But passion lends them power, time means, to meet,
      Tempering extremities with extreme sweet.

Scene one

A street beside the wall of Capulet's garden.

Enter ROMEO *walking away from* CAPULET'S *house.*

ROMEO
    Can I go forward when my heart is here?
    Turn back, dull earth, and find thy centre out.

He climbs over the wall into the garden.

Enter MERCUTIO *and* BENVOLIO *in the street.* ROMEO *listens from inside the garden.*

6 *conjure*   call; usually used for calling up spirits.

7 *humours*   moods.

11 *gossip*   friend, associate.

12 *purblind*   completely blind.

13 *Abraham Cupid*   it is not at all clear what Mercutio means here. There have been a number of suggestions: i) Abraham may mean old as Abraham in the Old Testament who was said to have lived to 175; ii) Abraham men was the name given to Elizabethan beggars and rascals, so it may mean rascal; iii) it may be a misreading for Adam Bell who was a famous archer at the time of Robin Hood. See also note to Act 1, scene 1, lines 169–70.

14 *King Cophetua . . . maid*   two characters in an old ballad, probably mentioned here as a reference to unsuitable or unlikely love matches.

15 *He*   Romeo.

16 *The ape . . . conjure him*   performing apes were trained to 'play dead' as a trick.

17 *conjure*   see note to line 6 above.

20 *demesnes*   surrounding areas; Mercutio is referring to her sexual organs.

23–7 *'T would anger . . . some spite*   Romeo would be angry if the spirit of another man were to come under her influence and therefore give Romeo a rival. The play on the words 'raise', 'mistress' circle', 'stand' and 'laid' are further examples of Mercutio's use of sexual innuendo.

BENVOLIO

Romeo! my cousin Romeo! Romeo!

MERCUTIO

                             He is wise,
And on my life hath stolen him to bed.

BENVOLIO

He ran this way and leapt this orchard wall.   5
Call, good Mercutio.

MERCUTIO

                    Nay, I'll conjure too.
Romeo! humours! madman! passion! liver!
Appear thou in the likeness of a sigh;
Speak but one rhyme and I am satisfied;
Cry but "Ay me", pronounce but "love" and
  "dove"   10
Speak to my gossip Venus one fair word,
One nickname for her purblind son and heir,
Young Abraham Cupid, he that shot so trim
When King Cophetua loved the beggar maid.
He heareth not, he stirreth not, he moveth not;   15
The ape is dead, and I must conjure him.
(*Addressing Romeo*) I conjure thee by Rosaline's
  bright eyes,
By her high forehead and her scarlet lip,
By her fine foot, straight leg and quivering thigh,
And the demesnes that there adjacent lie,   20
That in thy likeness thou appear to us.

BENVOLIO

And if he hear thee, thou wilt anger him.

MERCUTIO

This cannot anger him. 'T would anger him

27 *invocation*   spell, calling up.

29 *raise*   it was thought that spirits could be raised up, but here Mercutio continues to make sexual jokes.

31 *be consorted*   spend time with.

    humorous   full of humours, moody.

32 *hit the mark*   hit the target (again in a sexual sense).

34 *medlar tree*   bears apple-like fruit; here a pun on the word meddle, to interfere with, in this case, sexually.

38 *open-arse*   dialect for the fruit of the medlar but clearly a sexual reference too.

    Poperin pear   variety of pear but Mercutio is punning with the sound of the word 'Poperin'.

39 *truckle-bed*   low bed usually slept on by children which could be wheeled out of sight beneath a larger one. Mercutio is suggesting that his sleep will be like that of a child.

40 *field-bed*   make-shift bed out-of-doors.

Note: to bring this edition into line with most other editions, Act 2 is now divided into six scenes (instead of five). Scene 2 now starts after line 42 of scene 1.

---

1 *He*   Mercutio – Romeo has been listening to their conversation and comments that it is fine for Mercutio to mock love because he has never been in love himself.

To raise a spirit in his mistress' circle,
Of some strange nature, letting it there stand   25
Till she had laid it, and conjured it down;
That were some spite. My invocation
Is fair and honest: in his mistress' name
I conjure only but to raise up him.

BENVOLIO

Come; he hath hid himself among these trees   30
To be consorted with the humorous night;
Blind is his love, and best befits the dark.

MERCUTIO

If love be blind, love cannot hit the mark.
Now will he sit under a medlar tree,
And wish his mistress were that kind of fruit   35
As maids call medlars when they laugh alone.
O Romeo, that she were! O that she were
An open-arse and thou a Poperin pear!
Romeo, good night. I'll to my truckle-bed:
This field-bed is too cold for me to sleep.   40
Come, shall we go?

BENVOLIO

                    Go then, for 't is in vain.
To seek him here that means not to be found.

                    Exeunt MERCUTIO *and* BENVOLIO

Scene two

Inside Capulet's garden.

ROMEO

He jests at scars that never felt a wound.
(*He sees Juliet*) But soft! What light through yonder
    window breaks?

4 *envious*   jealous, because the moon is a symbol of chastity, but also because Juliet appears more beautiful than the moon itself.

7 *her maid*   Juliet is still a virgin.

7–9 *Be not . . . cast it off*   Romeo is trying to persuade Juliet that she should stop being chaste and be prepared to lose her virginity.

8 *vestal livery*   clothing worn by vestal virgins who served at Diana's (the moon goddess) temple.

13 *discourses*   speaks (not literally, but he suggests that her body language tells us what she is thinking).

17 *spheres*   the Ptolemaic system of astronomy showed the heavens as a series of crystal spheres, one inside the other, with the earth at the centre.

18 *they*   the stars.

21 *airy region*   sky.

29 *white-upturnèd*   looking upwards, so that the whites of the eyes show.

It is the east, and Juliet is the sun.
Arise, fair sun, and kill the envious moon,
Who is already sick and pale with grief   5
That thou her maid art far more fair than she.
Be not her maid, since she is envious;
Her vestal livery is but sick and green,
And none but fools do wear it; cast it off.
It is my lady, O it is my love!   10
O that she knew she were!
She speaks, yet she says nothing. What of that?
Her eye discourses: I will answer it.
I am too bold; 't is not to me she speaks.
Two of the fairest stars in all the heaven,   15
Having some business, do entreat her eyes
To twinkle in their spheres till they return.
What if her eyes were there, they in her head?
The brightness of her cheek would shame those
    stars
As daylight doth a lamp; her eyes in heaven   20
Would through the airy region stream so bright
That birds would sing and think it were not night.
See how she leans her cheek upon her hand.
O that I were a glove upon that hand,
That I might touch that cheek!

JULIET

                    Ay me!

ROMEO

                                She speaks.   25
O speak again, bright angel, for thou art
As glorious to this night, being o'er my head,
As is a wingèd messenger of heaven
Unto the white-upturnèd wondering eyes
Of mortals that fall back to gaze on him   30

33 *Wherefore*   why.

34 *refuse*   cast off.

35 *be but*   just be.

39 *though not*   even if you were not.

46 *owes*   has.

47 *doff*   throw off.

50 *new baptized*   I'll take that new name – names are bestowed at baptism.

52 *bescreened in night*   hidden by the darkness.

53 *counsel*   secret thoughts.

When he bestrides the lazy-pacing clouds,
And sails upon the bosom of the air.

JULIET

O Romeo, Romeo! Wherefore art thou Romeo?
Deny thy father and refuse thy name:
Or if thou wilt not, be but sworn my love   35
And I'll no longer be a Capulet.

ROMEO

(*Aside*) Shall I hear more, or shall I speak at this?

JULIET

'T is but thy name that is my enemy.
Thou art thyself, though not a Montague.
What's "Montague"? It is nor hand, nor foot,   40
Nor arm, nor face, nor any other part
Belonging to a man. O be some other name!
What's in a name? That which we call a rose
By any other word would smell as sweet.
So Romeo would, were he not Romeo called,   45
Retain that dear perfection which he owes
Without that title. Romeo, doff thy name,
And for that name, which is no part of thee,
Take all myself.

ROMEO

(*To* JULIET)   I take thee at thy word.
Call me but "Love", and I'll be new baptized;   50
Henceforth I never will be Romeo.

JULIET

What man art thou, that thus bescreened in night,
So stumblest on my counsel?

ROMEO

                              By a name

61 *thee dislike* displeases you.

62 *hither* here.

64 *death* the death of you.

66 *o'erperch* fly over.

67 *stony limits* walls.

69 *no stop* no bar.

71 *peril* danger.

72 *sweet* kindly.

73 *proof against their enmity* immune to their hatred.

I know not how to tell thee who I am.
My name, dear saint, is hateful to myself   55
Because it is an enemy to thee.
Had I it written, I would tear the word.

JULIET

My ears have yet not drunk a hundred words
Of thy tongue's uttering, yet I know the sound.
Art thou not Romeo, and a Montague?   60

ROMEO

Neither, fair maid, if either thee dislike.

JULIET

How camest thou hither, tell me, and wherefore?
The orchard walls are high and hard to climb,
And the place death, considering who thou art,
If any of my kinsmen find thee here.   65

ROMEO

With love's light wings did I o'erperch these walls,
For stony limits cannot hold love out;
And what love can do, that dares love attempt:
Therefore thy kinsmen are no stop to me.

JULIET

If they do see thee, they will murder thee.   70

ROMEO

Alack, there lies more peril in thine eye
Than twenty of their swords. Look thou but sweet
And I am proof against their enmity.

JULIET

I would not for the world they saw thee here.

ROMEO

I have night's cloak to hide me from their eyes.   75

76 *And but*   unless.

78 *proroguèd*   put off.

    wanting of   without.

81 *lent me counsel*   advised me.

82 *pilot*   navigator.

84 *I should . . . merchandise*   I would set out on this adventure to gain the rewards.

86 *Else*   or.

88 *Fain would I dwell on form*   I would happily speak as a lady should address a new lover.

89 *compliment*   politeness, convention.

92 *perjuries*   false promises.

93 *Jove*   king of the Roman gods and god of oaths who always laughed at lovers because their promises were so often broken.

96 *perverse*   awkward.

    say thee nay   say no to you.

97 *So thou wilt woo*   if you will go on wooing me.

99 *'haviour light*   behaviour irresponsible.

101 *strange*   aloof, distant, hard-to-get.

103 *ware*   aware.

And but thou love me, let them find me here;
My life were better ended by their hate
Than death proroguèd, wanting of thy love.

JULIET

By whose direction found'st thou out this place?

ROMEO

By love, that first did prompt me to inquire; 80
He lent me counsel, and I lent him eyes.
I am no pilot, yet wert thou as far
As that vast shore washed with the farthest sea,
I should adventure for such merchandise.

JULIET

Thou knowest the mask of night is on my face, 85
Else would a maiden blush bepaint my cheek,
For that which thou hast heard me speak tonight.
Fain would I dwell on form; fain, fain deny
What I have spoke: but farewell compliment!
Dost thou love me? I know thou wilt say "Ay", 90
And I will take thy word; yet if thou swear'st
Thou mayst prove false. At lovers' perjuries
They say Jove laughs. O gentle Romeo,
If thou dost love, pronounce it faithfully;
Or if thou think I am too quickly won,   95
I'll frown, and be perverse, and say thee nay,
So thou wilt woo; but else, not for the world.
In truth, fair Montague, I am too fond,
And therefore thou mayst think my 'haviour light.
But trust me, gentleman, I'll prove more true 100
Than those that have more cunning to be strange.
I should have been more strange, I must confess,
But that thou overheard'st, ere I was ware,
My true-love passion; therefore pardon me,

105 *And not impute . . . love*   do not think my love is trivial or shallow (or even immodest) because I give in to it so easily.

106 *discoverèd*   exposed.

109 *th' inconstant moon*   the moon was supposed to stand for unfaithfulness because it changes its shape as it waxes and wanes.

111 *likewise variable*   just as changeable.

114 *my idolatry*   my worship.

117 *contract*   lovers' agreement.

118 *unadvised*   badly thought out.

And not impute this yielding to light love,   105
Which the dark night hath so discoverèd.

ROMEO

Lady, by yonder blessèd moon I vow,
That tips with silver all these fruit-tree tops –

JULIET

O swear not by the moon, th' inconstant moon,
That monthly changes in her circled orb,   110
Lest that thy love prove likewise variable.

ROMEO

What shall I swear by?

JULIET

                              Do not swear at all;
Or if thou wilt, swear by thy gracious self,
Which is the god of my idolatry,
And I'll believe thee.

ROMEO

                              If my heart's dear love –   115

JULIET

Well, do not swear. Although I joy in thee,
I have no joy of this contract tonight:
It is too rash, too unadvised, too sudden,
Too like the lightning, which doth cease to be
Ere one can say "It lightens." Sweet, good night. 120
This bud of love, by summer's ripening breath,
May prove a beauteous flower when next we meet.
Good night, good night. As sweet repose and rest
Come to thy heart as that within my breast.

ROMEO

O wilt thou leave me so unsatisfied?   125

131 *frank*   generous.
133 *bounty*   what I have to give, generosity.
136 *adieu*   goodbye.
141 *substantial*   real.
143 *bent*   intention.

JULIET

What satisfaction canst thou have to-night?

ROMEO

Th' exchange of thy love's faithful vow for mine.

JULIET

I gave thee mine before thou didst request it;
And yet I would it were to give again.

ROMEO

Would'st thou withdraw it? For what purpose, love? 130

JULIET

But to be frank and give it thee again:
And yet I wish but for the thing I have.
My bounty is as boundless as the sea,
My love as deep; the more I give to thee,
The more I have, for both are infinite.   135

The NURSE *calls.*

I hear some noise within. Dear love, adieu.
(*To the* NURSE) Anon, good Nurse! (*To* ROMEO) Sweet
    Montague, be true.
Stay but a little; I will come again.

                    JULIET *leaves the window and goes in*

ROMEO

O blessed, blessed night! I am afeard,
Being in night, all this is but a dream,   140
Too flattering-sweet to be substantial.

JULIET *returns to the window.*

JULIET

Three words, dear Romeo, and good night indeed.
If that thy bent of love be honourable,

145 *procure*   authorise.

146 *rite*   wedding ceremony.

150 *But if thou mean'st not well*   if your intentions are not worthy.

151 *beseech*   beg, pray.

152 *cease thy suit*   stop courting me.

153 *thrive*   prosper.

155 *to want*   without.

Thy purpose marriage, send me word to-morrow
By one that I'll procure to come to thee,   145
Where and what time thou wilt perform the rite;
And all my fortunes at thy foot I'll lay,
And follow thee, my lord, throughout the world.

NURSE

(*From inside the house*) Madam!

JULIET

(*To the* NURSE) I come, anon. (*To* ROMEO) But if thou
    mean'st not well,   150
I do beseech thee –

NURSE

(*Calling again from within*) Madam!

JULIET

                By and by, I come –
(*Continuing, to* ROMEO) To cease thy suit, and leave
    me to my grief.
Tomorrow will I send.

ROMEO

              So thrive my soul, –

JULIET

A thousand times good night!

                        JULIET *goes in*

ROMEO

A thousand times the worse, to want thy light!   155
Love goes toward love as schoolboys from their
    books,
But love from love, toward school with heavy looks.

ROMEO *is walking away as* JULIET *returns.*

158–9   *Hist, Romeo . . . back again*   Juliet is trying to get Romeo to come back to her and she uses the language of falconry which was an extremely popular sport with the Elizabethan nobility. A 'tassel' was a highly-prized male peregrine falcon.

160   *Bondage is hoarse*   Juliet has to whisper because she is not free to go out of the house or to speak to men unless she is chaperoned. The secrecy of their meeting means that she cannot call out to him.

161   *Else would . . . Echo lies*   Echo was a nymph in Greek mythology who was condemned to speak only the last words anyone said to her. Because of this she couldn't tell Narcissus that she loved him. She lived in a cave until her body died and only her voice remained.

166   *attending*   listening.

172   *I shall forget*   I shall deliberately forget.

173   *Remembering*   thinking about.

JULIET

  Hist, Romeo, hist! O for a falconer's voice,
  To lure this tassel-gentle back again.
  Bondage is hoarse, and may not speak aloud,   160
  Else would I tear the cave where Echo lies,
  And make her airy tongue more hoarse than
    mine
  With repetition of my "Romeo!"

ROMEO

  It is my soul that calls upon my name.
  How silver-sweet sound lovers' tongues by night,   165
  Like softest music to attending ears.

JULIET

  Romeo!

ROMEO

      Madam?

JULIET

          What o'clock tomorrow
  Shall I send to thee?

ROMEO

             By the hour of nine.

JULIET

  I will not fail. 'T is twenty years till then.
  I have forgot why I did call thee back.   170

ROMEO

  Let me stand here till thou remember it.

JULIET

  I shall forget, to have thee still stand there,
  Remembering how I love thy company.

177 *wanton*   spoilt child.

179 *gyves*   ropes.

182 *I would I were*   I wish I were.

188 *ghostly sire*   father (in the sense of priest); here the Friar.

   close   hidden.

189 *dear hap*   good luck.

ROMEO

And I'll still stay, to have thee still forget,
Forgetting any other home but this.   175

JULIET

'T is almost morning. I would have thee gone,
And yet no farther than a wanton's bird,
Who lets it hop a little from her hand,
Like a poor prisoner in his twisted gyves,
And with a silk thread plucks it back again,   180
So loving-jealous of his liberty.

ROMEO

I would I were thy bird.

JULIET

                         Sweet, so would I,
Yet I should kill thee with much cherishing.
Good night, good night. Parting is such sweet
    sorrow,
That I shall say "good night" till it be morrow.   185

ROMEO

Sleep dwell upon thine eyes, peace in thy breast.
Would I were sleep and peace, so sweet to rest.

                                        JULIET *goes in*

Hence will I to my ghostly sire's close cell,
His help to crave, and my dear hap to tell.

                                        Exit

3 *fleckled* speckled with light.

4 *From forth* removed from.

Titan Hyperion was a god in Greek mythology (one of the Titans). He drove the sun chariot across the sky each day.

5 *advance* raises.

7 *osier cage* basket made of willow.

8 *baleful* poisonous.

10 *What . . . that* whatever is one is also the other.

11 *divers* various.

13 *Many . . . virtues excellent* many plants have many excellent virtues.

14 *None but for some* all possessing some goodness.

15 *mickle* great.

17 *nought* nothing.

19 *aught* anything.

strained from that fair use used in the wrong way.

22 *vice sometime by action dignified* good can sometimes come from evil.

23 *infant rind* delicate young skin.

25 *each part* every part of the body.

Scene three

FRIAR LAWRENCE'S *cell.*

Enter FRIAR LAWRENCE *with a basket.*

FRIAR LAWRENCE

The grey-eyed morn smiles on the frowning night,
Check'ring the eastern clouds with streaks of light;
And fleckled darkness like a drunkard reels
From forth day's path and Titan's fiery wheels.
Now, ere the sun advance his burning eye   5
The day to cheer and night's dank dew to dry,
I must upfill this osier cage of ours
With baleful weeds and precious-juicèd flowers.
The earth that's nature's mother is her tomb:
What is her burying grave, that is her womb,   10
And from her womb children of divers kind
We sucking on her natural bosom find:
Many for many virtues excellent,
None but for some, and yet all different.
O mickle is the powerful grace that lies   15
In plants, herbs, stones, and their true qualities:
For nought so vile that on the earth doth live
But to the earth some special good doth give;
Nor aught so good but, strained from that fair use,
Revolts from true birth, stumbling on abuse.   20
Virtue itself turns vice, being misapplied,
And vice sometime by action dignified.

Enter ROMEO, *unseen by the* FRIAR.

Within the infant rind of this weak flower
Poison hath residence and medicine power:
For this, being smelt, with that part cheers each
        part;   25

107

26 *stays* stops, arrests.

28 *grace and rude will* God's grace and goodness and the passion which rules all human beings.

29 *the worser* passion.

30 *canker* canker worm which devours plants.

31 *Benedicite* (Latin) bless you. The audience is immediately aware that Romeo is talking to a friar.

33–4 *it argues . . . thy bed* it shows you are worried to have got up so early.

37 *unbruisèd* not battered by experience.

   unstuffed carefree, unworried.

38 *Doth couch his limbs* lies down.

40 *uproused* out of bed.

   distemperature discomfort, worry.

46 *woe* unhappiness.

Being tasted, stays all senses with the heart.
Two such opposèd kings encamp them still
In man as well as herbs, grace and rude will;
And where the worser is predominant,
Full soon the canker death eats up that plant.　　30

ROMEO

Good morrow, father.

FRIAR LAWRENCE
　　　　　　　Benedicite.
What early tongue so sweet saluteth me?
Young son, it argues a distempered head
So soon to bid good morrow to thy bed.
Care keeps his watch in every old man's eye,　　35
And where care lodges, sleep will never lie;
But where unbruisèd youth with unstuffed brain
Doth couch his limbs, there golden sleep doth reign.
Therefore thy earliness doth me assure
Thou art uproused with some distemperature;　　40
Or if not so, then here I hit it right,
Our Romeo hath not been in bed to-night.

ROMEO

That last is true: the sweeter rest was mine.

FRIAR LAWRENCE

God pardon sin! Wast thou with Rosaline?

ROMEO

With Rosaline, my ghostly father? No.　　45
I have forgot that name, and that name's woe.

FRIAR LAWRENCE

That's my good son. But where hast thou been
　　then?

50 *on a sudden* suddenly.

one of my enemies (i.e. Juliet).

51–2 *Both our remedies . . . physic lies* we can both be cured by the same medicine. This metaphor compares religious comfort to medicine.

54 *intercession* prayer.

steads assists.

55 *homely in thy drift* clear in what you mean.

56 *Riddling . . . shrift* if you do not make it plain what you are confessing to you will not find the penance easy to fathom either.

60 *all combined* we are in complete agreement.

63 *pass* walk along together.

65 *St Francis* Lawrence is a Franciscan friar and he swears here by the founder and patron saint of his order.

67 *forsaken* abandoned.

68 *in their eyes* they go only by appearances and beauty.

69 *brine* salt water, tears.

70 *sallow* pale.

72 *season* flavour or preserve – meats were preserved with seasoning.

ROMEO

I'll tell thee ere thou ask it me again:
I have been feasting with mine enemy,
Where on a sudden one hath wounded me   50
That's by me wounded. Both our remedies
Within thy help and holy physic lies.
I bear no hatred, blessed man, for lo,
My intercession likewise steads my foe.

FRIAR LAWRENCE

Be plain, good son, and homely in thy drift;   55
Riddling confession finds but riddling shrift.

ROMEO

Then plainly know, my heart's dear love is set
On the fair daughter of rich Capulet:
As mine on hers, so hers is set on mine,
And all combined, save what thou must combine   60
By holy marriage. When and where and how
We met, we wooed, and made exchange of vow,
I'll tell thee as we pass, but this I pray,
That thou consent to marry us to-day.

FRIAR LAWRENCE

Holy Saint Francis, what a change is here!   65
Is Rosaline that thou didst love so dear
So soon forsaken? Young men's love then lies
Not truly in their hearts, but in their eyes.
Jesu Maria, what a deal of brine
Hath washed thy sallow cheeks for Rosaline!   70
How much salt water thrown away in waste
To season love, that of it doth not taste!
The sun not yet thy sighs from heaven clears,
Thy old groans ring yet in mine ancient ears;
Lo, here upon thy cheek the stain doth sit   75

111

79 *Pronounce this sentence then*   repeat after me. (The friar is teasing Romeo about his sudden change of heart.)

80 *Women may fall . . .men*   women can be forgiven for being unfaithful when men are not faithful.

81 *chid'st*   chastised, told me off.

82 *doting*   being infatuated.

83 *bad'st*   told me to.

86 *allow*   return.

88 *Thy love did read by rote*   Rosaline knew very well that you could speak about love off by heart, as if you had learned how from a book, rather than really felt or understood it.

90 *In one respect*   for one reason.

92 *rancour*   bitterness.

93 *stand on*   insist on.

Of an old tear that is not washed off yet.
If e'er thou wast thyself, and these woes thine,
Thou and these woes were all for Rosaline.
And art thou changed? Pronounce this sentence then:
Women may fall, when there's no strength in men. 80

ROMEO
Thou chid'st me oft for loving Rosaline.

FRIAR LAWRENCE
For doting, not for loving, pupil mine.

ROMEO
And bad'st me bury love.

FRIAR LAWRENCE
     Not in a grave
To lay one in, another out to have.

ROMEO
I pray thee chide me not. Her I love now   85
Doth grace for grace and love for love allow:
The other did not so.

FRIAR LAWRENCE
    O she knew well
Thy love did read by rote that could not spell.
But come, young waverer, come go with me;
In one respect I'll thy assistant be,   90
For this alliance may so happy prove
To turn your households' rancour to pure love.

ROMEO
O let us hence. I stand on sudden haste.

FRIAR LAWRENCE
Wisely and slow. They stumble that run fast.

Exeunt

1 *should* can.

2 *to-night* last night.

3 *his man* Romeo's servant.

10 *answer it* rise to the challenge.

12 *how he dares* by saying that he dares.

14 *already dead* killed by love.

16 *pin* centre.

Scene four

A street.

Enter MERCUTIO *and* BENVOLIO.

MERCUTIO
Where the devil should this Romeo be? Came he not
home to-night?

BENVOLIO
Not to his father's; I spoke with his man.

MERCUTIO
Why, that same pale hard-hearted wench, that
Rosaline, torments him so, that he will sure run   5
mad.

BENVOLIO
Tybalt, the kinsman to old Capulet, hath sent a letter to his father's house.

MERCUTIO
A challenge, on my life.

BENVOLIO
Romeo will answer it.   10

MERCUTIO
Any man that can write may answer a letter.

BENVOLIO
Nay, he will answer the letter's master, how he
dares, being dared.

MERCUTIO
Alas, poor Romeo, he is already dead – stabbed
with a white wench's black eye, run through the ear   15
with a love song, the very pin of his heart cleft with

115

18 *blind bowboy's butt shaft* Cupid's arrow. (See also note to Act 1, scene 1, lines 169–70.)

20 *Prince of Cats* cats were often called 'Tyb' in Shakespeare's time (like the modern cat's name 'Tibby').

21 *captain of compliments* master in clever swordfighting and formal duelling. The whole of the speech that follows revolves around swordplay and its timing, terms which are akin to musical notation ('time', 'distance', 'proportion', 'minim rests').

24 *butcher of a silk button* he can spear your buttons on the point of his sword because he is so skilful and accurate.

25–6 *very first house* foremost school (of duelling).

26 *first and second cause* two stages in duelling.

27 *passado* forward thrust.

punto reverso back-handed thrust.

hai scoring blow.

29 *The pox of . . . affecting fantasticoes* a curse on such ridiculous, lisping, affected dandies. Mercutio is mocking Tybalt for being a follower of the Continental style of duelling which was very fashionable at the time, though scorned by some.

30 *new tuners of accent* people who use the latest slang words.

31 *blade* swordsman.

tall brave.

33 *strange flies* foreign parasites, pests.

34 *pardon-me's* people who are overly formal and polite, but are insincere.

34–6 *fashion-mongers . . . old bench?* some people rely so much on the new way of going about things that they cannot rest with the old ways. Notice Mercutio's punning: a 'form' is another name for a bench, and those who stand cannot sit at ease.

38 *without his roe* a roe deer is female so Mercutio is pointing out that he is without a girlfriend. 'Ro' is also the first part of his name, so he may mean that Romeo is only half himself. Lastly, roes are the eggs of fish and so Romeo is weak like a fish that has just spawned – this leads into a new set of puns for Mercutio.

39 *numbers* verses.

the blind bowboy's butt shaft. And is he a man to
encounter Tybalt?

BENVOLIO

Why, what is Tybalt?

MERCUTIO

More than Prince of Cats. O, he's the courageous 20
captain of compliments. He fights as you sing prick-
song, – keeps time, distance, and proportion: he
rests me his minim rests – one, two, and the third in
your bosom. The very butcher of a silk button, a
duellist, a duellist, a gentleman of the very first 25
house of the first and second cause. Ah, the immortal passado, the punto reverso, the hai!

BENVOLIO

The what?

MERCUTIO

The pox of such antic, lisping, affecting fantasticoes,
these new tuners of accent! "By Jesu, a very good 30
blade! a very tall man! a very good whore!" Why, is
not this a lamentable thing, grandsire, that we
would be thus afflicted with these strange flies, these
fashion-mongers, these "pardon-me's" who stand
so much on the new form that they cannot sit at ease 35
on the old bench? O, their bones, their bones!

Enter ROMEO.

BENVOLIO

Here comes Romeo, here comes Romeo.

MERCUTIO

Without his roe, like a dried herring. O flesh, flesh,
how art thou fishified! Now is he for the numbers

40 *Petrarch* Italian poet who invented the 14-line sonnet form when writing to Laura, the woman he loved.

to his lady compared with Rosaline. Mercutio still thinks Romeo is in love with her.

41-2 *she had a better love to be-rhyme her* Laura had a better poet to write verses to her.

42 *Dido* Queen of Carthage, loved Aeneas the founder of Rome.

Cleopatra Queen of Egypt, loved Mark Antony.

43 *Helen* Queen of Sparta, stolen away by Paris to Troy.

Hero Greek beauty, loved by Lysander.

hildings and harlots sluts and whores.

Thisbe loved by Pyramus.

43-4 *a grey eye* grey eyes were thought to be attractive to the Elizabethans, however Mercutio may be punning again on the Greek mythological Graiei, three hideous hags with only a single eye between them.

44 *not to the purpose* it doesn't matter.

45-6 *to your French slop* to go with your baggy trousers. (Romeo has not yet changed out of his party clothes.)

46 *gave us the counterfeit* gave us the slip, disappeared.

49 *slip* fake coin, but to give someone the slip is to escape or run away from them.

51-2 *strain courtesy* forget his manners.

53-4 *constrains . . . the hams* compels a man to bend his legs – Mercutio is implying that Romeo has spent all night making love to Rosaline.

56 *most kindly hit it* understood it very well.

58 *pink* small flower and so perfection, but also the centre or soul.

that Petrarch flowed in! Laura to his lady was a 40
kitchen wench – marry, she had a better love to be-
rhyme her – Dido a dowdy, Cleopatra a gipsy,
Helen and Hero hildings and harlots, Thisbe a grey
eye or so, but not to the purpose. Signior Romeo,
bonjour! There's a French salutation to your French 45
slop. You gave us the counterfeit fairly last night.

ROMEO

Good morrow to you both. What counterfeit did I
give you?

MERCUTIO

The slip, sir, the slip. Can you not conceive?

ROMEO

Pardon, good Mercutio. My business was great, 50
and in such a case as mine a man may strain courtesy.

MERCUTIO

That's as much as to say, such a case as yours constrains a man to bow in the hams.

ROMEO

Meaning to curtsy?   55

MERCUTIO

Thou hast most kindly hit it.

ROMEO

A most courteous exposition.

MERCUTIO

Nay, I am the very pink of courtesy.

ROMEO

Pink for flower?

61 *pump well-flowered*   shoe ornamented with pinked (serrated-edged) holes.

64–5 *solely singular*   unique.

66 *single-soled*   thin, poor.

singleness   stupidity.

67 *Come between us*   break this duel of words up; I can't keep up with it.

68–9 *Switch . . . a match*   beat your wits to make them go faster, spur them on, otherwise I win.

70 *wild-goose chase*   pointless chase.

71 *wild-goose*   foolish person.

73 *Was I with you there*   did you get my point?

75 *there for the goose*   playing the fool, clowning around.

76 *I will bite . . . jest*   biting the ear was a sign of affection.

MERCUTIO

Right.   60

ROMEO

Why, then is my pump well-flowered.

MERCUTIO

Sure wit! Follow me this jest now till thou hast worn
out thy pump, that when the single sole of it is
worn, the jest may remain, after the wearing, solely
singular.   65

ROMEO

O single-soled jest, solely singular for the singleness!

MERCUTIO

Come between us, good Benvolio; my wits faints.

ROMEO

Switch and spurs, switch and spurs! or I'll cry a
match.

MERCUTIO

Nay, if our wits run the wild-goose chase, I am 70
done, for thou hast more of the wild-goose in one of
thy wits than, I am sure, I have in my whole five.
Was I with you there for the goose?

ROMEO

Thou wast never with me for anything when thou
wast not there for the goose.   75

MERCUTIO

I will bite thee by the ear for that jest.

ROMEO

Nay, good goose, bite not.

78–9 *bitter sweeting* bitter and sweet, funny and painful at the same time. Bittersweet apples were made into sauce to serve with goose.

80 *is it not . . . goose?* Romeo says that his sharp wit goes well with the sweet fool, Mercutio.

81 *cheveril* goat skin which stretches easily.

82 *inch* 2.5cm.

ell 110cm.

83 *broad* used in the sense of crude, thus Romeo is saying that Mercutio is a dirty-minded fool.

88 *by art* by skill.

89 *natural* foolish person.

90 *lolling* with its tongue hanging out.

bauble jester's stick (but Mercutio is probably also referring to male genitals, and in the following lines to the sexual act).

92 *against the hair* when I don't want to. 'Hare' was also a slang word for prostitute.

94 *large* lewd, rude.

97 *occupy the argument* carry on with the story.

MERCUTIO

Thy wit is a very bitter sweeting; it is a most sharp
sauce.

ROMEO

And is it not well served in to a sweet goose?   80

MERCUTIO

O here's a wit of cheveril, that stretches from an
inch narrow to an ell broad!

ROMEO

I stretch it out for that word "broad", which, added
to the "goose", proves thee far and wide a broad
goose.   85

MERCUTIO

Why, is not this better now than groaning for love?
Now art thou sociable; now art thou Romeo; now
art thou what thou art, by art as well as by nature.
For this drivelling love is like a great natural that
runs lolling up and down to hide his bauble in a   90
hole.

BENVOLIO

Stop there, stop there.

MERCUTIO

Thou desirest me to stop in my tale against the hair.

BENVOLIO

Thou wouldst else have made thy tale large.

MERCUTIO

O thou art deceived. I would have made it short, for   95
I was come to the whole depth of my tale, and
meant indeed to occupy the argument no longer.

98 *goodly gear* a fine spectacle.

A sail the Nurse looks like a ship approaching on the horizon, presumably because of her smock.

99 *a shirt and a smock* a man and a woman.

105 *God ye* God give you.

106 *e'en* see note to Act 1, scene 2, line 57.

109 *prick* point, but Mercutio is aiming to shock the Nurse with the obscene double meaning.

110 *Out upon you!* get away with you! The Nurse is pretending to be shocked by Mercutio.

Enter NURSE *and her man* PETER.

ROMEO

Here's goodly gear! A sail, a sail!

MERCUTIO

Two, two! a shirt and a smock.

NURSE

Peter!   100

PETER

Anon.

NURSE

My fan, Peter.

MERCUTIO

Good Peter, to hide her face, for her fan's the fairer
face.

NURSE

God ye good morrow, gentlemen.   105

MERCUTIO

God ye good e'en, fair gentlewoman.

NURSE

Is it good e'en?

MERCUTIO

'T is no less, I tell ye, for the bawdy hand of the dial
is now upon the prick of noon.

NURSE

Out upon you! What a man are you?   110

ROMEO

One, gentlewoman, that God hath made, for himself to mar.

113 *By my troth* upon my word, a mild swear word.

114 *quoth 'a?* did he say?

118 *fault* want.

123 *confidence* the Nurse may mean that she wishes to speak to Romeo in confidence or privately, or she may have mistaken the word 'conference'.

124 *endite* invite.

125 *A bawd* pimp, one who provides clients for a prostitute.

   So ho! huntsman's cry.

127 *Hare* i) the animal, ii) a slang word for prostitute.

   a lenten pie pie made without any meat during the fasting period of Lent.

128 *hoar* stale or mouldy.

   spent devoured, finished.

NURSE

By my troth, it is well said. "For himself to mar,"
quoth 'a? Gentlemen, can any of you tell me where I
may find the young Romeo?   115

ROMEO

I can tell you, but young Romeo will be older when
you have found him than he was when you sought
him. I am the youngest of that name, for fault of a
worse.

NURSE

You say well.   120

MERCUTIO

Yea, is the worst well? Very well took, i' faith; wisely
wisely.

NURSE

If you be he, sir, I desire some confidence with you.

BENVOLIO

She will endite him to some supper.

MERCUTIO

A bawd, a bawd, a bawd! So ho!   125

ROMEO

What, hast thou found?

MERCUTIO

No hare, sir, unless a hare, sir, in a lenten pie that is
something stale and hoar ere it be spent.

He sings.

> An old hare hoar,
> And an old hare hoar,   130
> Is very good meat in Lent:

133 *too much for a score*   not worth paying for.

134 *hoars*   double meaning: turns mouldy or spends time with prostitutes (whores).

139 *saucy merchant*   rude person.

140 *ropery*   rudeness.

2–3 *stand to*   live up to (or be sexually aroused).

144 *take him down*   sort him out, get one up on him.

145 *and 'a were*   even if he were.

146 *Jacks*   rude ruffians.

147 *Scurvy*   vile.

   flirt-gills   easy woman, loose woman.

148 *skainsmates*   meaning unclear, possibly scapegrace – a graceless, hare-brained
   fellow. The Nurse takes exception to Mercutio and accuses him of having
   dubious friends.

149 *suffer*   allow.

1–4 *I saw no man . . . on my side*   Peter's answer is vague, but seems to suggest,
   on one level that he would defend her in a duel, and on another that he is as
   ready as the next man for sexual activity.

But a hare that is hoar
Is too much for a score,
When it hoars ere it be spent.

Romeo will you come to your father's? We'll to 135
dinner thither.

ROMEO

I will follow you.

MERCUTIO

Farewell, ancient lady; farewell, lady, lady, lady.

Exeunt MERCUTIO *and* BENVOLIO

NURSE

I pray you, sir, what saucy merchant was this that
was so full of his ropery?   140

ROMEO

A gentleman, Nurse, that loves to hear himself talk,
and will speak more in a minute than he will stand
to in a month.

NURSE

And 'a stand to anything against me, I'll take him
down and 'a were lustier than he is, and twenty 145
such Jacks; and if I cannot, I'll find those that shall.
Scurvy knave! I am none of his flirt-gills, I am none
of his skainsmates. (*To Peter*) And thou must stand
by, too, and suffer every knave to use me at his
pleasure!   150

PETER

I saw no man use you at his pleasure. If I had, my
weapon should quickly have been out. I warrant
you, I dare draw as soon as another man if I see
occasion in a good quarrel, and the law on my side.

155 *vexed* annoyed.

160–1 *lead her into a fool's paradise* lead her astray with empty promises of marriage.

163 *deal double* cheat her.

165 *weak dealing* sly, underhand way of behaving.

166 *commend me* speak kindly of me.

167 *protest* promise.

170 *mark* hear.

174 *shrift* confession.

176 *Be shrived* be forgiven her sins following her confession.

177 *for thy pains* for your trouble.

NURSE

Now, afore God, I am so vexed that every part ab- 155
out me quivers. (*Referring to* MERCUTIO) Scurvy
knave! (*To* ROMEO) Pray you, sir, a word. And, as I
told you, my young lady bid me inquire you out.
What she bid me say I will keep to myself; but first
let me tell ye, if ye should lead her into a fool's para- 160
dise, as they say, it were a very gross kind of behaviour, as they say; for the gentlewoman is young,
and therefore, if you should deal double with her,
truly it were an ill thing to be offered to any gentlewoman, and very weak dealing.   165

ROMEO

Nurse, commend me to thy lady and mistress. I
protest unto thee –

NURSE

Good heart! and i' faith I will tell her as much.
Lord, Lord, she will be a joyful woman!

ROMEO

What wilt thou tell her, Nurse? Thou dost not mark 170
me.

NURSE

I will tell her, sir, that you do protest, which, as I
take it, is a gentlemanlike offer.

ROMEO

Bid her devise some mèans to come to shrift this
    afternoon,
And there she shall, at Friar Lawrence's cell,   175
Be shrived and married. (*He offers her money*) Here is
    for thy pains.

180 *stay*   wait.

182 *a tackled stair*   rope ladder.

183 *topgallant*   highest point (literally a small mast fixed to the tall topmast of a sailing ship).

184 *convey*   means of travel.

185 *quit*   reward.

189 *secret*   to be trusted (meaning Romeo's manservant).

190 *putting one away*   as long as no third person is listening (the other two may keep a secret).

191 *I warrant thee*   I assure you.

193 *'t*   Juliet. The Nurse often refers to her as 'it'.

   prating   chattering.

194 *would fain lay knife aboard*   would like to claim her as his own.

195 *as lief*   would rather.

NURSE

No, truly, sir; not a penny.

ROMEO

Go to, I say you shall.

NURSE

(*Taking the money*) This afternoon, sir? Well, she
shall be there.

ROMEO

And stay, good Nurse, behind the abbey wall: 180
Within this hour my man shall be with thee,
And bring thee cords made like a tackled stair,
Which to the high topgallant of my joy
Must be my convoy in the secret night.
Farewell. Be trusty, and I'll quit thy pains.   185
Farewell. Commend me to thy mistress.

NURSE

Now God in heaven bless thee! Hark you, sir.

ROMEO

What say'st thou, my dear Nurse?

NURSE

Is your man secret! Did you ne'er hear say,
"Two may keep counsel, putting one away"?   190

ROMEO

I warrant thee my man's as true as steel.

NURSE

Well, sir. My mistress is the sweetest lady. Lord,
Lord! when 't was a little prating thing – O, there is
a nobleman in town, one Paris, that would fain lay
knife aboard, but she, good soul, had as lief see a 195
toad, a very toad, as see him. I anger her, some-

199   *clout*   piece of fabric.

      versal   entire.

199–200 *Rosemary*   herb used at weddings and funerals, a symbol of remembrance.

200   *a letter*   the same letter.

202   *dog-name*   R sounds like the growl a dog might make.

      R is for the   we do not know what the Nurse is about to say but can probably guess at 'arse', which sounds as if it might begin with an 'R'.

204   *sententious*   she means to say sentences (another malapropism).

209   *Before and apace*   go on ahead of me and hurry up.

times, and tell her that Paris is the properer man,
but I'll warrant you, when I say so, she looks as pale
as any clout in the versal world. Doth not "rosemary and "Romeo" begin with a letter?   200

ROMEO
Ay, Nurse, what of that? Both with an R.

NURSE
Ah, mocker, that's the dog-name. R is for the – No,
I know it begins with some other letter; and she
hath the prettiest sententious of it, of you and
rosemary, that it would do you good to hear it.   205

ROMEO
Commend me to thy lady.

NURSE
Ay, a thousand times. Peter!

PETER
Anon.

NURSE
Before, and apace.

Exeunt

Scene five

The Capulets' garden.

Enter JULIET.

JULIET
The clock struck nine when I did send the Nurse;
In half an hour she promised to return.

3 *Perchance she cannot*   maybe, perhaps by chance she is unable.
   not so   not possible.
6 *louring*   dark and threatening, scowling.
7 *nimble-pinioned*   swift-winged.
   draw Love   draw him along in his chariot.
8 *wind-swift*   as fast as the wind.
14 *bandy*   pass (like knocking a ball or shuttlecock gently between two people).
16 *feign as*   pretend to be.
25 *Give me leave*   let me be on my own.
26 *jaunce*   merry dance, rigmarole.

Perchance she cannot meet him – that's not so.
O, she is lame! Love's heralds should be thoughts,
Which ten times faster glides than the sun's beams   5
Driving back shadows over louring hills.
Therefore do nimble-pinioned doves draw Love,
And therefore hath the wind-swift Cupid wings.
Now is the sun upon the highmost hill
Of this day's journey, and from nine to twelve   10
Is three long hours, yet she is not come.
Had she affections and warm youthful blood,
She would be as swift in motion as a ball:
My words would bandy her to my sweet love,
And his to me.   15
But old folks – many feign as they were dead:
Unwieldy, slow, heavy, and pale as lead.

Enter PETER *followed by* NURSE.

O God, she comes! – O honey Nurse, what news?
Hast thou met with him? Send thy man away.

NURSE
Peter, stay at the gate.   20

Exit PETER

JULIET
Now good sweet Nurse – O Lord, why lookest thou
     sad?
Though news be sad, yet tell them merrily:
If good, thou shamest the music of sweet news
By playing it to me with so sour a face.

NURSE
I am aweary; give me leave a while.   25
Fie, how my bones ache! What a jaunce have I!

137

29 *stay* wait.

34 *excuse* make excuses for not telling.

36 *stay the circumstance* wait until later to hear the full details.

38 *simple* naive, silly.

42 *be not to be talked on* are not worth mentioning.

43 *flower of courtesy* most gentlemanly.

44–5 *Go thy ways, wench; serve God* go and get on with what you should be doing and be a good girl.

49 *as* as though.

50 *a' t'* on the.

JULIET

I would thou hadst my bones, and I thy news.
Nay, come, I pray thee, speak; good, good Nurse,
  speak.

NURSE

Jesu, what haste! Can you not stay a while?
Do you not see that I am out of breath?   30

JULIET

How art thou out of breath, when thou hast breath
To say to me that thou art out of breath?
The excuse that thou dost make in this delay
Is longer than the tale thou dost excuse.
Is thy news good or bad? Answer to that.   35
Say either, and I'll stay the circumstance.
Let me be satisfied; is 't good or bad?

NURSE

Well, you have made a simple choice; you know not
how to choose a man. Romeo? No, not he. Though
his face be better than any man's, yet his leg excels 40
all men's; and for a hand and a foot and a body,
though they be not to be talked on, yet they are past
compare. He is not the flower of courtesy, but, I'll
warrant him, as gentle as a lamb. Go thy ways,
wench; serve God. What, have you dined at home? 45

JULIET

No, no. But all this did I know before.
What says he of our marriage? What of that?

NURSE

Lord, how my head aches! What a head have I!
It beats as it would fall in twenty pieces.
My back a' t' other side; ah, my back, my back!   50

51 *Beshrew your heart* you should be ashamed of yourself.

53 *I' faith* in faith, honestly.

55 *honest* respectable, decent.

61 *God's Lady* mild swear word referring to the Virgin Mary.

62 *hot* eager; amorous.

Marry, come up, I trow the Nurse is getting impatient with Juliet for being so demanding and tells her to ease up a little.

63 *poultice* remedy, cure (literally a cloth placed on a wound).

64 *Henceforth* from now on.

65 *coil* to-do, fuss.

66 *leave* permission.

68 *hie you hence* off you go.

69 *stays* waits.

70 *wanton* unrestrained.

Beshrew your heart for sending me about
To catch my death with jauncing up and down.

JULIET

I' faith, I am sorry that thou art not well.
Sweet, sweet, sweet Nurse, tell me, what says my
   love?

NURSE

Your love says, like an honest gentleman, and a 55
courteous, and a kind, and a handsome, and, I warrant, a virtuous – Where is your mother?

JULIET

Where is my mother? Why, she is within.
Where should she be? How oddly thou repliest:
"Your love says, like an honest gentleman,   60
'Where is your mother?'"

NURSE

                    O God's Lady dear!
Are you so hot? Marry, come up, I trow.
Is this the poultice for my aching bones?
Henceforth do your messages yourself.

JULIET

Here's such a coil! Come, what says Romeo?   65

NURSE

Have you got leave to go to shrift to-day?

JULIET

I have.

NURSE

Then hie you hence to Friar Lawrence' cell;
There stays a husband to make you a wife.
Now comes the wanton blood up in your cheeks: 70

71 *be in scarlet straight*   immediately blush.

72 *I must another way*   I must go somewhere else.

74 *bird's nest*   Juliet is like a bird which must return to her nest – or bed – at night, where Romeo will visit her.

75–6 *I am the drudge . . . soon at night*   at the moment I am your servant working for your pleasure; soon you will have to take this responsibility for yourself. 'Bear the burden' also suggests she will carry her husband's weight on her in love-making.

78 *high fortune*   when watching tragedies the Elizabethan audience would have known that the point of 'high fortune' was the turning point of the story which had up to now been full of promise.

1 *So smile the heavens*   may the heavens (God) look kindly.

2 *after-hours . . . us not*   and not send sadness in the future as a rebuke.

3 *come what sorrow can*   whatever sad things happen now.

4 *countervail*   counterbalance, equal (and therefore reduce).

exchange of joy   the happiness given in return.

6 *Do thou*   if you will only.

close our . . . words   join our hands in holy matrimony.

7 *do*   may do.

8 *but*   only.

9–11 *These violent delights . . . consume*   the Friar suggests that lovers' passions are exciting, but short-lived, like fire or gunpowder. They are used up quickly through the contact of the lovers. His reference to 'violent ends' reminds us of the fate of Romeo and Juliet which we are told of in the Prologue to Act 1.

12 *loathsome in his own deliciousness*   tastes sickly because it is so sweet.

They'll be in scarlet straight at any news.
Hie you to church; I must another way,
To fetch a ladder, by the which your love
Must climb a bird's nest soon when it is dark.
I am the drudge, and toil in your delight,   75
But you shall bear the burden soon at night.
Go. I'll to dinner; hie you to the cell.

JULIET
Hie to high fortune! Honest Nurse, farewell.

Exeunt

Scene six

Friar Lawrence's cell.

Enter FRIAR LAWRENCE *and* ROMEO.

FRIAR LAWRENCE
So smile the heavens upon this holy act
That after-hours with sorrow chide us not.

ROMEO
Amen, amen. But come what sorrow can,
It cannot countervail the exchange of joy
That one short minute gives me in her sight.   5
Do thou but close our hands with holy words,
Then love-devouring death do what he dare;
It is enough I may but call her mine.

FRIAR LAWRENCE
These violent delights have violent ends,
And in their triumph die like fire and powder,   10
Which, as they kiss, consume. The sweetest honey
Is loathsome in his own deliciousness,

143

13 *confounds*   spoils, destroys.

14 *long*   long-lasting.

15 *Too swift . . . slow*   variation on the proverb 'More haste, less speed'.

18 *bestride the gossamers*   ride on spiders' webs.

19 *idles*   drifts.

19–20 *That idles so light is vanity*   the Friar is pointing out that the dreamy lovers are so wrapped up in themselves that they cannot come down to earth. He is also implying the fragility of love.

21 *ghostly*   spiritual.

23 *As much . . . much*   Juliet must kiss Romeo in return or she will be in debt to him.

24–9 *if the measure . . . dear encounter*   if you have as much love as I do, and are better at telling others about it, then speak of it now and let the music of your voice reveal how happy we are because of this meeting.

30–1 *Conceit*   imagination.

substance   reality.

ornament   artificiality, adornment.

32 *can count their worth*   put a value on what they have.

34 *I cannot sum up sum*   I cannot begin to add up.

And in the taste confounds the appetite.
Therefore love moderately; long love doth so:
Too swift arrives as tardy as too slow.   15

Enter JULIET.

Here comes the lady. O, so light a foot
Will ne'er wear out the everlasting flint.
A lover may bestride the gossamers
That idles in the wanton summer air,
And yet not fall, so light is vanity.   20

JULIET
Good even to my ghostly confessor.

FRIAR LAWRENCE
Romeo shall thank thee, daughter, for us both.

ROMEO *kisses her.*

JULIET
As much to him, else is his thanks too much.

She returns his kiss.

ROMEO
Ah, Juliet, if the measure of thy joy
Be heaped like mine, and that thy skill be more 25
To blazon it, then sweeten with thy breath
This neighbour air, and let rich music's tongue
Unfold the imagined happiness that both
Receive in either, by this dear encounter.

JULIET
Conceit more rich in matter than in words   30
Brags of his substance, not of ornament.
They are but beggars that can count their worth,
But my true love is grown to such excess
I cannot sum up sum of half my wealth.

35 *make short work*   not take long.
36 *by your leaves*   with the permission of both of you.
37 *incorporate*   join together.

FRIAR LAWRENCE

Come, come with me, and we will make short work;   35
For, by your leaves, you shall not stay alone
Till Holy Church incorporate two in one.

Exeunt

Act 3: summary

The hot weather is making everyone in Verona irritable. Tybalt, out looking for a quarrel with Romeo, meets Mercutio and Benvolio. Mercutio challenges him and another sword-fight breaks out. Both of the youths are excellent fencers and a match for one another, so it is only when Romeo steps between them to part them that a mistake is made and Mercutio is fatally wounded. Romeo cannot control his grief at his friend's death and he sets off after Tybalt, killing him in return. The Prince, however, cannot bear to bring a harsher sentence than banishment on Romeo, who was acting in his own kinsman's interest.

When the Nurse brings news of Tybalt's death to Juliet she is heartbroken for her cousin but is misled into believing for a while that Romeo has also been killed. When she discovers the truth she realises that she may not see Romeo again after that night and sends the Nurse to find him.

Romeo is hiding with Friar Lawrence when the Nurse arrives and together they plan to smuggle Juliet from Verona to Mantua where Romeo will wait for her. Meanwhile, Capulet and Paris arrange the wedding in an attempt to make Juliet forget her cousin's death.

At dawn on Tuesday Romeo and Juliet bid one another farewell just before Lord and Lady Capulet come to tell her of the wedding plans. Juliet defies them, refusing to marry Paris, and making her father very angry with her. Juliet is confused, her Nurse unsympathetic, so she sets out to beg help from Friar Lawrence.

*(Opposite) The Nurse and Juliet: Young Vic Company production of **Romeo and Juliet**, London 1982 (© Christopher Pearce).*

2 *Capels* Capulets.

3 *scape* avoid.

4 *these hot...stirring* the hot weather is making everyone cross and irritable.

6 *claps me* throws down before me.

8 *by the operation...cup* as soon as he has finished his second drink (having had too much).

8–9 *draws him on the drawer* draws his sword at the waiter.

11 *as hot a Jack* as angry a ruffian.

12 *moved to be moody* angered.

13 *moody to be moved* ready to be made angry.

15 *and there were two such* if there were two of you.

Act Three

A street.

Enter MERCUTIO, *his* PAGE, BENVOLIO *and* SERVANTS.

BENVOLIO

    I pray thee, good Mercutio, let's retire:
    The day is hot, the Capels are abroad,
    And if we meet we shall not scape a brawl,
    For now, these hot days, is the mad blood stirring.

MERCUTIO

    Thou art like one of these fellows that, when he en-   5
    ters the confines of a tavern, claps me his sword
    upon the table and says, "God send me no need of
    thee"; and by the operation of the second cup draws
    him on the drawer, when indeed there is no need.

BENVOLIO

    Am I like such a fellow?   10

MERCUTIO

    Come, come; thou art as hot a Jack in thy mood as
    any in Italy, and as soon moved to be moody, and
    as soon moody to be moved.

BENVOLIO

    And what to?

MERCUTIO

    Nay, and there were two such, we should have none 15
    shortly, for one would kill the other. Thou? Why,
    thou wilt quarrel with a man that hath a hair more

20 *hazel*   the colour of his eyes but referring also to hazel nuts.

23 *meat*   nourishment.

24 *addle*   rotten.

27 *fall out*   argue with.

28 *doublet*   jacket. Easter was traditionally a time when new clothes were worn. This was an action which could not be expected to cause offence.

29 *riband*   ribbon or laces.

30 *tutor me*   teach me, advise me.

31 *And*   if.

31–3 *any man should...and a quarter*   no one would buy my life expecting it to last longer than an hour and a quarter.

34 *O, simple!*   what a stupid thing to say.

35 *By my head*   an oath or swear word.

36 *By my heel*   Mercutio invents his own swear word, punning on that used by Benvolio. It also suggests he intends to stay and fight, not run away (take to his heels).

or a hair less in his beard than thou hast. Thou wilt
quarrel with a man for cracking nuts, having no
other reason but because thou hast hazel eyes. 20
What eye but such an eye would spy out such a
quarrel? Thy head is as full of quarrels as an egg is
full of meat, and yet thy head hath been beaten as
addle as an egg for quarrelling. Thou last quarrelled
with a man for coughing in the street because he 25
hath wakened thy dog that hath lain asleep in the
sun. Didst thou not fall out with a tailor for wearing
his new doublet before Easter? With another for
tying his new shoes with old riband? And yet thou
wilt tutor me from quarrelling! 30

BENVOLIO
And I were so apt to quarrel as thou art, any man
should buy the fee-simple of my life for an hour and
a quarter.

MERCUTIO
The fee-simple? O, simple!

Enter TYBALT *and his followers.*

BENVOLIO
By my head, here comes the Capulets! 35

MERCUTIO
By my heel, I care not.

TYBALT
(*To his followers*) Follow me close, for I will speak to
    them.
(*To* MERCUTIO *and* BENVOLIO) Gentlemen, good e'en;
    a word with one of you.

39 *Couple it*   match it.

41 *apt*   ready.

41–2 *and you will give me occasion*   if you give me a reason.

44 *consortest*   are friends with, go around with. Mercutio picks up on this rather pompous word in the next line.

45 *Consort*   group of musicians. Mercutio chooses to take offence at this because minstrels or musicians were servants.

47 *fiddlestick*   sword (as if it were the bow for a violin).

48 *Zounds*   by God's (or Christ's) wounds (a strong swear word).

49 *public haunt*   place where the public are allowed, i.e. in the street.

51 *reason coldly*   speak sensibly, rationally.

55 *my man*   the man I want to speak to (i.e. Romeo). Again Mercutio takes 'man' to mean servant.

56 *your livery*   your servant's uniform.

MERCUTIO

And but one word with one of us? Couple it with
something: make it a word and a blow.   40

TYBALT

You shall find me apt enough to that, sir, and you
will give me occasion.

MERCUTIO

Could you not take some occasion without giving?

TYBALT

Mercutio, thou consortest with Romeo –

MERCUTIO

Consort? What, dost thou make us minstrels? And 45
thou make minstrels of us, look to hear nothing but
discords. Here's my fiddlestick; here's that shall
make you dance. Zounds, consort!

BENVOLIO

We talk here in the public haunt of men.
Either withdraw unto some private place,   50
Or reason coldly of your grievances,
Or else depart. Here, all eyes gaze on us.

MERCUTIO

Men's eyes were made to look, and let them gaze.
I will not budge for no man's pleasure, I.

Enter ROMEO.

TYBALT

(*To* MERCUTIO) Well, peace be with you, sir; here
comes my man.   55

MERCUTIO

But I'll be hanged, sir, if he wear your livery.

57 *to field*   to the duelling field.

58 *Your worship*   a respectful title, but Mercutio is being sarcastic and mocking Tybalt.

59 *bear*   feel towards.

    afford   offer.

61 *reason...love thee*   Tybalt and Romeo are now kinsmen because of the latter's recent marriage to Juliet, thus Romeo has reason to love him.

62 *excuse the appertaining rage*   reduce the anger I would normally have felt towards you.

65 *Boy*   by belittling Romeo, Tybalt is insulting him.

68 *devise*   guess.

70 *tender*   respect.

73 *'Alla stoccata' carries it away*   Tybalt wins the day (because Romeo has given in). Mercutio is referring to Tybalt by a fencing term, and he has already talked about Tybalt's prowess and affectation in swordplay – see note to Act 2, scene 3, line 21 on.

74 *walk*   step this way (to a place where we can duel).

76 *King of Cats*   see note to Act 2, scene 3, line 20.

76–7 *nine lives*   cats are said to be lucky enough to have nine lives.

77–8 *I mean to...eight*   I will do what I want with your first life (of the nine) and then, depending how you treat me afterwards, I shall use up your other eight by giving you a beating.

Marry, go before to field, he'll be your follower:
Your worship in that sense may call him "man".

TYBALT

Romeo, the love I bear thee can afford
No better term than this: thou art a villain.   60

ROMEO

Tybalt, the reason that I have to love thee
Doth much excuse the appertaining rage
To such a greeting. Villain am I none;
Therefore, farewell; I see thou know'st me not.

TYBALT

Boy, this shall not excuse the injuries   65
That thou hast done me; therefore turn and draw.

ROMEO

I do protest I never injured thee,
But love thee better than thou can'st devise
Till thou shalt know the reason of my love.
And so, good Capulet, which name I tender   70
As dearly as mine own, be satisfied.

MERCUTIO

O calm, dishonourable, vile submission!
"Alla stoccata" carries it away.
(*He draws his sword*) Tybalt, you rat-catcher, will you
    walk?

TYBALT

What would'st thou have with me?   75

MERCUTIO

Good King of Cats, nothing but one of your nine
lives that I mean to make bold withal, and, as you
shall use me hereafter, dry-beat the rest of the eight.

79 *his pilcher*   its scabbard.

81 *I am for you*   I am ready to fight you.

82 *put thy rapier up*   put your sword away.

83 *passado*   lunge.

86 *forbear*   put an end to.

88 *bandying*   fighting.

90 *A plague o' both your houses!*   a curse on both of your families.

I am sped   finished, killed.

91 *hath nothing*   has no wounds.

Will you pluck your sword out of his pilcher by the
ears? Make haste, lest mine be about your ears ere it   80
be out.

TYBALT

(*Drawing his sword*) I am for you.

ROMEO

Gentle Mercutio, put thy rapier up.

MERCUTIO

(*To* TYBALT) Come, sir, your passado.

MERCUTIO *and* TYBALT *fight.*

ROMEO

Draw, Benvolio; beat down their weapons.   85
Gentlemen, for shame, forbear this outrage!
Tybalt! Mercutio! the Prince expressly hath
Forbid this bandying in Verona streets.
Hold, Tybalt! good Mercutio!

Romeo comes between them. TYBALT *wounds* MERCUTIO *from
behind* ROMEO, *then runs away, followed by his men.*

MERCUTIO

　　　　　　　　I am hurt.
A plague o' both your houses! I am sped.   90
Is he gone, and hath nothing?

BENVOLIO

　　　　　　　　What, art thou hurt?

MERCUTIO

Ay, ay, a scratch, a scratch; marry, 't is enough.
Where is my page? Go, villain, fetch a surgeon.

Exit PAGE

96 *serve* be enough (to kill him).

97 *grave* solemn but also buried in a grave. Even though he is dying Mercutio continues to make puns.

98 *peppered* run through, fatally wounded.

100 *braggart* boaster, someone who brags.

101 *by the book of arithmetic* by the rules.

107 *worms' meat* a corpse.

109 *near ally* close relation.

111 *In* on.

112 *slander* spoken insult.

an hour for only an hour (i.e. since his marriage to Juliet made them relations).

115 *And in my...valour's steel* my loving mood has softened my courage (tempering steel makes it hard).

ROMEO

    Courage, man; the hurt cannot be much.

MERCUTIO

    No, 't is not so deep as a well, nor so wide as a   95
church door, but 't is enough, 't will serve. Ask for
me to-morrow and you shall find me a grave man. I
am peppered, I warrant, for this world. A plague, o'
both your houses! Zounds! a dog, a rat, a mouse, a
cat, to scratch a man to death! A braggart, a rogue, 100
a villain that fights by the book of arithmetic! Why
the devil came you between us? I was hurt under
your arm.

ROMEO

    I thought all for the best.

MERCUTIO

    Help me into some house, Benvolio,   105
Or I shall faint. A plague o' both your houses!
They have made worms' meat of me. I have it,
And soundly too. Your houses!

BENVOLIO *helps him out.*

ROMEO

    This gentleman, the Prince's near ally,
My very friend, hath got this mortal hurt   110
In my behalf, my reputation stained
With Tybalt's slander – Tybalt that an hour
Hath been my cousin. O sweet Juliet,
Thy beauty hath made me effeminate,
And in my temper softened valour's steel.   115

BENVOLIO *returns.*

BENVOLIO

    O Romeo, Romeo, brave Mercutio is dead.

117 *aspired* risen up to.

118 *untimely* early, before its time.

119 *on more...depend* threatens the future.

123 *respective lenity* lenience or tolerance born out of respect. Up until now Romeo
has been careful not to get drawn into a fight with Tybalt. Mercutio's death,
however, changes this.

124 *conduct* guide or behaviour.

128 *Staying* waiting.

130 *consort* keep company with.

131 *Shalt with him hence* will go the same way as he did.

133 *up* alerted to what has happened.

134 *Stand not amazed...taken* do not stand there in a trance; the Prince will pass
the death sentence on you if you are caught.

136 *fortune's fool* a toy for Fate to play with.

That gallant spirit hath aspired the clouds,
Which too untimely here did scorn the earth.

ROMEO

This day's black fate on more days doth depend;
This but begins the woe others must end.　　　　120

TYBALT *returns*.

BENVOLIO

Here comes the furious Tybalt back again.

ROMEO

Alive, in triumph! and Mercutio slain!
Away to heaven, respective lenity,
And fire-eyed fury be my conduct now!
Now, Tybalt, take the "villain" back again　　　125
That late thou gavest me, for Mercutio's soul
Is but a little way above our heads,
Staying for thine to keep him company.
Either thou or I, or both, must go with him.

TYBALT

Thou, wretched boy, that did consort him here,　　130
Shalt with him hence.

ROMEO

(*Drawing his sword*)　　This shall determine that.

They fight, and ROMEO *kills* TYBALT.

BENVOLIO

Romeo, away, be gone!
The citizens are up, and Tybalt slain.
Stand not amazed: the Prince will doom thee death
If thou art taken. Hence, be gone, away!　　　135

ROMEO

O, I am fortune's fool.

140 *charge* order.
142 *discover* tell.
143 *manage* events.
148 *true* just.

BENVOLIO

> Why dost thou stay?

> *Exit* ROMEO

Enter an OFFICER *and* CITIZENS.

OFFICER

Which way ran he that killed Mercutio?
Tybalt, that murderer, which way ran he?

BENVOLIO

There lies that Tybalt.

OFFICER

> Up, sir, go with me:

I charge thee in the Prince's name, obey.   140

Enter PRINCE ESCALUS, MONTAGUE, CAPULET, *their wives and
servants.*

PRINCE

Where are the vile beginners of this fray?

BENVOLIO

O noble Prince, I can discover all
The unlucky manage of this fatal brawl.
There lies the man, slain by young Romeo,
That slew thy kinsman, brave Mercutio.   145

LADY CAPULET

Tybalt, my cousin! O my brother's child!
O Prince! O cousin! husband! O the blood is spilled
Of my dear kinsman. Prince, as thou art true,
For blood of ours, shed blood of Montague.
O cousin, cousin!   150

PRINCE

Benvolio, who began this bloody fray?

153 *spoke him fair*   was polite to him.

   bethink   think.

154 *nice*   unimportant.

   urged withal   spoke strongly about too.

157 *take truce with*   make peace with.

   unruly spleen   uncontrolled rage (the spleen was thought to be the seat of anger in the body).

160 *all as hot*   just as fired up (with anger).

161 *martial scorn*   Mercutio's anger was sneering and he behaved in a warlike, aggressive way.

163–4 *dexterity Retorts it*   skill returns it.

171 *entertained*   thought of, considered.

177 *Affection makes him false*   his love for Romeo makes him lie.

BENVOLIO

Tybalt, here slain, whom Romeo's hand did slay.
Romeo, that spoke him fair, bid him bethink
How nice the quarrel was, and urged withal
Your high displeasure. All this, utterèd   155
With gentle breath, calm look, knees humbly
    bowed,
Could not take truce with the unruly spleen
Of Tybalt, deaf to peace, but that he tilts
With piercing steel at bold Mercutio's breast,
Who, all as hot, turns deadly point to point,   160
And, with a martial scorn, with one hand beats
Cold death aside, and with the other sends
It back to Tybalt, whose dexterity
Retorts it. Romeo – he cries aloud,
"Hold, friends! friends part!" and, swifter than his
    tongue,   165
His agile arm beats down their fatal points,
And 'twixt them rushes, underneath whose arm
An envious thrust from Tybalt hit the life
Of stout Mercutio, and then Tybalt fled,
But by and by comes back to Romeo,   170
Who had but newly entertained revenge,
And to 't they go like lightning, for, ere I
Could draw to part them, was stout Tybalt slain,
And as he fell, did Romeo turn and fly.
This is the truth, or let Benvolio die.   175

LADY CAPULET

He is a kinsman to the Montague.
Affection makes him false; he speaks not true.
Some twenty of them fought in this black strife,
And all those twenty could but kill one life.
I beg for justice, which thou, Prince, must give: 180
Romeo slew Tybalt; Romeo must not live.

185 *His fault...end*   although in the wrong, his crime is only to have killed the man whom the law would have condemned to death anyway (for Mercutio's murder).

187 *exile*   banish him from the city.

189 *My blood*   my relation.

190 *amerce*   punish.

193 *purchase out abuses*   pay for your crimes (and therefore cancel them out).

197 *Mercy but...kill*   pardoning killers only leads to more people being killed because there is no deterrent in mercy.

1 *apace*   quickly.

2 *Phoebus'*   the sun's.

waggoner   driver.

3 *Phaeton*   in mythology the son of Apollo. Phaeton asked Apollo if he might drive the sun chariot through the sky. Reluctantly Apollo allowed it but Phaeton could not control the horses and the runaway chariot plunged from the sky, killing him and bringing nightfall early.

PRINCE
    Romeo slew him; he slew Mercutio.
    Who now the price of his dear blood doth owe?

MONTAGUE
    Not Romeo, Prince; he was Mercutio's friend.
    His fault concludes but what the law should end – 185
    The life of Tybalt.

PRINCE
              And for that offence
    Immediately we do exile him hence.
    I have an interest in your hate's proceedings:
    My blood for your rude brawls doth lie a-bleeding.
    But I'll amerce you with so strong a fine   190
    That you shall all repent the loss of mine.
    I will be deaf to pleading and excuses;
    Nor tears, nor prayers shall purchase out abuses.
    Therefore use none. Let Romeo hence in haste,
    Else when he is found, that hour is his last.   195
    Bear hence this body, and attend our will.
    Mercy but murders, pardoning those that kill.

                        Exeunt

Scene two

Juliet's room.

Enter JULIET

JULIET
    Gallop apace, you fiery-footed steeds,
    Towards Phoebus' lodging! Such a waggoner
    As Phaeton would whip you to the west,
    And bring in cloudy night immediately.

5 *love-performing night*   night will not consummate their love, but it will take place under cover of night.

6 *runaway's*   Juliet may be referring back to Phaeton: see note to line 3 on page 168.

   wink   sleep, and thus ignore.

8 *amorous*   loving.

10 *best agrees with*   suits.

   civil   civilised, kindly.

12–13 *learn me how...maidenhoods*   teach me, now that I have won Romeo, how to lose my virginity along with his.

14 *Hood...cheeks*   hide the blushes rising to my cheeks (she compares her passionate love to an untamed falcon).

15 *mantle*   cloak (of darkness).

15–16 *till strange...modesty*   until what is new to me becomes familiar and I no longer need be shy about physical love.

17 *day in night*   Romeo, who is like a light shining at night, making it seem like daytime.

21 *die*   in Elizabethan times this also referred to sexual ecstasy.

25 *garish*   too bright, gaudy.

26–8 *O, I have...enjoyed*   she and Romeo, although married, have not yet made love. Juliet speaks as if she is exchanging contracts on property.

Spread thy close curtain, love-performing night;   5
That runaway's eyes may wink, and Romeo
Leap to these arms untalked of and unseen.
Lovers can see to do their amorous rites
By their own beauties; or, if love be blind
It best agrees with night. Come, civil night,   10
Thou sober-suited matron all in black,
And learn me how to lose a winning match,
Played for a pair of stainless maidenhoods.
Hood my unmanned blood, bating in my cheeks,
With thy black mantle, till strange love, grown
   bold,   15
Think true love acted simple modesty.
Come, night; come, Romeo; come, thou day in
   night,
For thou wilt lie upon the wings of night,
Whiter than new snow upon a raven's back.
Come, gentle night; come, loving, black-browed
   night,   20
Give me my Romeo; and when I shall die,
Take him and cut him out in little stars,
And he will make the face of heaven so fine
That all the world will be in love with night
And pay no worship to the garish sun.   25
O, I have bought the mansion of a love,
But not possessed it; and though I am sold,
Not yet enjoyed. So tedious is this day
As is the night before some festival
To an impatient child that hath new robes   30
And may not wear them. O here comes my Nurse,

Enter NURSE *with the rope ladder.*

And she brings news; and every tongue that speaks
But Romeo's name, speaks heavenly eloquence.

34 *cords* rope ladder (see Act 2, scene 3, lines 182–4).

37 *well-a-day* an expression of grief.

38 *undone* ruined.

39 *envious* malicious, cruel.

45–50 *Say thou but 'Ay'... 'No'* it is important to remember that for Elizabethan audiences, puns were not always meant to add humour; here Juliet appears confused and distracted.

47 *cockatrice* mythical beast, a cross between a cockerel and a snake, which could kill its prey just by looking at it.

51 *weal or woe* joy or grief.

Now, Nurse, what news? What hast thou there? The cords
  The cords
That Romeo bid thee fetch?

NURSE

                    Ay, ay, the cords.   35

JULIET

Ay me, what news? Why dost thou wring thy
  hands?

NURSE

Ah, well-a-day! He's dead, he's dead, he's dead!
We are undone, lady, we are undone.
Alack the day, he's gone, he's killed, he's dead!

JULIET

Can heaven be so envious?

NURSE

                  Romeo can,   40
Though heaven cannot. O Romeo, Romeo!
Whoever would have thought it? Romeo!

JULIET

What devil art thou dost torment me thus?
This torture should be roared in dismal hell.
Hath Romeo slain himself? Say thou but "Ay", 45
And that bare vowel "I" shall poison more
Than the death-darting eye of cockatrice.
I am not I, if there be such an "I",
Or those eyes shut that makes thee answer "Ay".
If he be slain, say "Ay", or if not, "No".   50
Brief sounds determine my weal or woe.

NURSE

I saw the wound, I saw it with mine eyes –

54 *corse*   dead body.

55 *bedaubed*   painted with.

56 *gore*   clotted.

    swounded   fainted, swooned.

57–60 *O break...bier!*   Juliet thinks that Romeo is dead and so wishes to die too.

57 *bankrupt*   without possessions (in this case, without love rather than money).

59 *Vile earth*   Juliet's body.

    to earth resign   sink into the grave.

60 *press...bier*   rest in a single grave.

64 *contrary*   one way and then the other.

67 *general doom*   the end of the world, of everything.

73 *A serpent...face*   devil's heart hidden behind a handsome face. The devil tempted Eve in the garden of Eden in the shape of a serpent. Romeo looks beautiful but is evil because he has killed Tybalt.

74 *Did ever...cave*   dragons in legend guarded their treasures, which they hoarded in caves.

God save the mark! – here on his manly breast;
A piteous corse, a bloody, piteous corse;
Pale, pale as ashes, all bedaubed in blood,   55
All in gore blood; I swounded at the sight.

JULIET

O break, my heart! poor bankrupt, break at once!
To prison, eyes; ne'er look on liberty!
Vile earth, to earth resign, end motion here,
And thou and Romeo press one heavy bier!   60

NURSE

O Tybalt, Tybalt, the best friend I had!
O courteous Tybalt, honest gentleman,
That ever I should live to see thee dead!

JULIET

What storm is this that blows so contrary?
Is Romeo slaughtered, and is Tybalt dead?   65
My dearest cousin, and my dearer lord?
Then, dreadful trumpet, sound the general doom,
For who is living if those two are gone?

NURSE

Tybalt is gone and Romeo banishèd;
Romeo that killed him, he is banishèd.   70

JULIET

O God! did Romeo's hand shed Tybalt's blood?

NURSE

It did, it did! alas the day, it did!

JULIET

O serpent heart, hid with a flowering face!
Did ever dragon keep so fair a cave?
Beautiful tyrant, fiend angelical,   75

77 *Despisèd substance...show* anything which appears beautiful but is actually evil underneath.

81 *bower* hide within a beautiful arbour.

86 *perjured* are false, have lied.

87 *naught* nothing (or evil).

dissemblers cheats, hiding the truth.

88 *aqua-vitae* brandy or other strong spirit (to revive her).

95 *chide* scold, speak ill of.

98 *poor my* my poor.

smooth speak well of.

Dove-feathered raven, wolvish-ravening lamb,
Despisèd substance of divinest show,
Just opposite to what thou justly seem'st,
A damnèd saint, an honourable villain!
O nature, what hadst thou to do in hell   80
When thou didst bower the spirit of a fiend
In mortal paradise of such sweet flesh?
Was ever book containing such vile matter
So fairly bound? O that deceit should dwell
In such a gorgeous palace!

NURSE

                    There's no trust,   85
No faith, no honesty in men; all perjured,
All forsworn, all naught, all dissemblers.
Ah, where's my man? Give me some aqua-vitae.
These griefs, these woes, these sorrows make me
   old.
Shame come to Romeo!

JULIET

                  Blistered be thy tongue   90
For such a wish! He was not born to shame.
Upon his brow shame is ashamed to sit,
For 't is a throne where honour may be crowned
Sole monarch of the universal earth.
O what a beast was I to chide at him!   95

NURSE

Will you speak well of him that killed your cousin?

JULIET

Shall I speak ill of him that is my husband?
Ah, poor my lord, what tongue shall smooth thy
   name,
When I, thy three-hours' wife, have mangled it?

102 *native spring* where you came from.

103–4 *You tributary...joy* you should be tears of grief but instead you are tears of joy (because she realises Romeo has not been killed).

109 *fain* happily, willingly.

110 *to* on.

116 *fellowship* company.

117 *needly will be* has to be.

120 *Which modern...moved* I would have felt the usual grief, rather than this more unusual kind I feel because Romeo is banished.

121 *with a rearward* coming up behind, hard on the heels.

123 *Is* is the same as.

126 *that word's death* the death which the word 'banished' suggests.

sound describe adequately.

But wherefore, villain, didst thou kill my cousin?   100
That villain cousin would have killed my husband.
Back, foolish tears, back to your native spring;
Your tributary drops belong to woe,
Which you, mistaking, offer up to joy.
My husband lives, that Tybalt would have slain,   105
And Tybalt's dead that would have slain my hus-
    band.
All this is comfort. Wherefore weep I then?
Some word there was, worser than Tybalt's death,
That murdered me. I would forget it fain,
But O, it presses to my memory   110
Like damnèd guilty deeds to sinners' minds:
"Tybalt is dead, and Romeo banishèd."
That "banishèd", that one word "banishèd",
Hath slain ten thousand Tybalts. Tybalt's death
Was woe enough if it had ended there;   115
Or, if sour woe delights in fellowship
And needly will be ranked with other griefs,
Why followed not, when she said, "Tybalt's dead",
"Thy father", or "thy mother", nay, or both,
Which modern lamentation might have moved?   120
But with a rearward following Tybalt's death,
"Romeo is banishèd"! To speak that word
Is father, mother, Tybalt, Romeo, Juliet,
All slain, all dead. "Romeo is banishèd".
There is no end, no limit, measure, bound,   125
In that word's death; no words can that woe sound.
Where is my father and my mother, Nurse?

NURSE
    Weeping and wàiling over Tybalt's corse.
    Will you go to them? I will bring you thither.

132 *beguiled* tricked.
139 *wot* know.

1 *fearful* frightened, scared.
2–3 *Affliction...calamity* suffering is in love with you and you are married to
misfortune.

JULIET

    Wash they his wounds with tears? Mine shall be
       spent   130
    When theirs are dry, for Romeo's banishment.
    Take up those cords. Poor ropes, you are beguiled,
    Both you and I, for Romeo is exiled.
    He made you for a highway to my bed,
    But I, a maid, die maiden-widowèd.   135
    Come, cords; come Nurse; I'll to my wedding bed,
    And death, not Romeo, take my maidenhead.

NURSE

    Hie to your chamber. I'll find Romeo
    To comfort you; I wot well where he is.
    Hark ye, your Romeo will be here at night: 140
    I'll to him; he is hid at Lawrence' cell.

JULIET

    O find him! Give this ring to my true knight,
    And bid him come to take his last farewell.

                                            Exeunt

Scene three

Friar Lawrence's cell.

Enter FRIAR LAWRENCE.

FRIAR LAWRENCE

    Romeo, come forth; come forth, thou fearful man.
    Affliction is enamoured of thy parts,
    And thou art wedded to calamity.

ROMEO *comes forward from the inner room.*

4 *doom*   judgement.

9 *doomsday*   the end of the world, in other words Romeo thinks the Prince will condemn him to death.

10 *vanished*   came.

18 *purgatory*   according to the Catholic doctrine, the place between heaven and hell where souls wait in suffering for their crimes before they are allowed into heaven.

21 *mis-termed*   under another name.

22 *cuts't...axe*   you give me hope and then take it away again.

24 *deadly sin*   mortal sin – an evil doing for which you cannot expect forgiveness. The Friar believes Romeo should be grateful for his punishment being less than death.

ROMEO

Father, what news? What is the Prince's doom?
What sorrow craves acquaintance at my hand   5
That I yet know not?

FRIAR LAWRENCE

                    Too familiar
Is my dear son with such sour company:
I bring thee tidings of the Prince's doom.

ROMEO

What less than doomsday is the Prince's doom?

FRIAR LAWRENCE

A gentler judgement vanished from his lips: 10
Not body's death, but body's banishment.

ROMEO

Ha, banishment? Be merciful, say "death",
For exile hath more terror in his look,
Much more, than death; do not say "banishment".

FRIAR LAWRENCE

Hence from Verona art thou banishèd.   15
Be patient, for the world is broad and wide.

ROMEO

There is no world without Verona walls,
But purgatory, torture, hell itself.
Hence "banishèd" is banished from the world,
And world's exile is death. Then "banishèd"   20
Is death mis-termed. Calling death "banishèd",
Thou cut'st my head off with a golden axe,
And smilest upon the stroke that murders me.

FRIAR LAWRENCE

O deadly sin! O rude unthankfulness!

25 *fault*   crime.

 calls   punishes by.

26 *rushed*   brushed, swept.

28 *dear*   precious and rare.

33 *validity*   value.

34 *courtship*   courtly behaviour, wooing.

35 *carrion flies*   flies which feed on rotting corpses.

37 *immortal blessing*   kisses or kind words.

38 *vestal*   virginal.

44 *sharp-ground*   sharpened on a grindstone.

45 *sudden mean*   quick method.

 ne'er so mean   however base or dishonourable.

49 *divine*   a holy man, a priest.

51 *mangle*   torture.

52 *fond*   foolish.

Thy fault our law calls death, but the kind Prince, 25
Taking thy part, hath rushed aside the law,
And turned that black word "death" to "banish-
     ment".
This is dear mercy, and thou seest it not.

ROMEO
'T is torture and not mercy. Heaven is here
Where Juliet lives, and every cat and dog   30
And little mouse, every unworthy thing,
Live here in heaven and may look on her,
But Romeo may not. More validity,
More honourable state, more courtship, lives
In carrion flies than Romeo: they may seize   35
On the white wonder of dear Juliet's hand,
And steal immortal blessing from her lips,
Who even in pure and vestal modesty
Still blush, as thinking their own kisses sin,
But Romeo may not; he is banishèd.   40
Flies may do this, but I from this must fly;
They are free men, but I am banishèd.
And say'st thou yet that exile is not death?
Hadst thou no poison mixed, no sharp-ground
     knife,
No sudden mean of death, though ne'er so mean,   45
But "banishèd" to kill me? "Banishèd"!
O Friar, the damnèd use that word in hell;
Howling attends it. How hast thou the heart,
Being a divine, a ghostly confessor,
A sin-absolver, and my friend professed,   50
To mangle me with that word "banishèd"?

FRIAR LAWRENCE
Thou fond madman, hear me a little speak.

55 *Adversity*   bad luck.

57 *Yet*   still.

59 *Displant*   uproot and move.

60 *prevails not*   accomplishes nothing.

63 *dispute with*   discuss.

   estate   position.

67 *Doting*   loving madly, infatuated.

70 *Taking the measure...grave*   measuring out the size of my own grave.

ROMEO

O thou wilt speak again of banishment.

FRIAR LAWRENCE

I'll give thee armour to keep off that word:
Adversity's sweet milk, philosophy,   55
To comfort thee though thou art banishèd.

ROMEO

Yet "banishèd"? Hang up philosophy!
Unless philosophy can make a Juliet,
Displant a town, reverse a Prince's doom,
It helps not, it prevails not, talk no more.   60

FRIAR LAWRENCE

O, then I see that madmen have no ears.

ROMEO

How should they, when that wise men have no eyes?

FRIAR LAWRENCE

Let me dispute with thee of thy estate.

ROMEO

Thou canst not speak of that thou dost not feel.
Wert thou as young as I, Juliet thy love,   65
An hour but married, Tybalt murderèd,
Doting like me, and like me banishèd,
Then mightst thou speak, then mightst thou tear
     thy hair,
And fall upon the ground as I do now,
Taking the measure of an unmade grave.   70

ROMEO *flings himself on the floor. There is knocking at the door.*

FRIAR LAWRENCE

Arise; one knocks. Good Romeo, hide thyself.

73 *infold*   hide.
75 *taken*   caught.
84 *even in my mistress' case*   is behaving just like my mistress.

ROMEO

Not I, unless the breath of heartsick groans
Mist-like infold me from the search of eyes.

More knocking.

FRIAR LAWRENCE

Hark, how they knock! – Who's there? – Romeo,
    arise;
Thou wilt be taken. – (*He calls*) Stay a while! –
    (*To* ROMEO) Stand up!   75
Run to my study. – (*He calls*) By and by! –
    (*To* ROMEO) God's will,
What simpleness is this? – (*He calls*) I come, I come!

Louder knocking.

Who knocks so hard? Whence come you? What's
    your will?

NURSE

(*From outside*) Let me come in, and you shall know
    my errand.
I come from Lady Juliet.

FRIAR LAWRENCE

(*Opening the door*)   Welcome then.   80

NURSE

(*Entering*) O holy Friar, O tell me, holy Friar,
Where's my lady's lord? Where's Romeo?

FRIAR LAWRENCE

There on the ground, with his own tears made
    drunk.

NURSE

O he is even in my mistress' case,

90 *O* grief (the shape of a wailing mouth).

93 *old* hardened.

94 *childhood* early days.

95 *removed but little* closely related.

97 *concealed* hidden (in the sense that it is not generally known that Juliet is his wife).

102 *level* aim.

)6–7 *sack the hateful mansion* destroy (ransack) the hated place (i.e. his own body).

Just in her case. O woeful sympathy!   85
Piteous predicament! Even so lies she,
Blubbering and weeping, weeping and blubbering.
(*To* ROMEO) Stand up, stand up! Stand, and you be a
    man!
For Juliet's sake; for her sake rise and stand.
Why should you fall into so deep an O?   90

ROMEO
(*Rising*) Nurse!

NURSE
                    Ah Sir! Ah sir! Death's the end of all.

ROMEO
Spak'st thou of Juliet? How is it with her?
Doth she not think me an old murderer,
Now I have stained the childhood of our joy
With blood removed but little from her own?   95
Where is she? and how doth she? and what says
My concealed lady to our cancelled love?

NURSE
O she says nothing, sir, but weeps and weeps,
And now falls on her bed, and then starts up,
And Tybalt calls, and then on Romeo cries,   100
And then down falls again.

ROMEO
                    As if that name,
Shot from the deadly level of a gun,
Did murder her as that name's cursèd hand
Murdered her kinsman. O tell me, Friar, tell me,
In what vile part of this anatomy   105
Doth my name lodge? Tell me, that I may sack
The hateful mansion.

108 *form*   appearance, shape.

109 *denote*   show, point to.

110 *unreasonable*   unreasoning.

112 *ill-beseeming...both*   in behaving like a man and a woman at the same time you are like some unnatural wild animal.

113 *amazed*   astounded.

114 *I thought...tempered*   I thought your personality was more balanced.

117 *But*   by.

damnèd hate   committing suicide, a sin punishable in the eyes of God with eternal hell.

118 *rail'st*   curse.

121 *shape*   manliness.

22–3 *like a usurer...use indeed*   like a miser you have a great deal (in Romeo's case, manhood, love, intelligence) but you don't use any of it properly.

125 *form of wax*   a mere copy – easily melted.

126 *digressing from*   in moving away from, by not showing.

127 *hollow perjury*   empty lies.

31–2 *Like powder...ignorance*   like the gunpowder a foolish soldier carries to fire his gun, you explode (into passion and grief) because of your own ignorance.

133 *dismembered*   blown limb from limb.

thine own defence   the very thing that should protect you.

He draws his dagger to kill himself, but the NURSE *snatches it from him.*

FRIAR LAWRENCE
                  Hold thy desperate hand!
Art thou a man? Thy form cries out thou art:
Thy tears are womanish, thy wild acts denote
The unreasonable fury of a beast.   110
Unseemly woman in a seeming man,
And ill-beseeming beast in seeming both!
Thou hast amazed me. By my holy order,
I thought thy disposition better tempered.
Hast thou slain Tybalt? Wilt thou slay thyself?   115
And slay thy lady, that in thy life lives,
But doing damnèd hate upon thyself?
Why rail'st thou on thy birth, the heaven, and
    earth,
Since birth, and heaven, and earth, all three, do
    meet
In thee at once, which thou at once would'st lose? 120
Fie, fie! Thou sham'st thy shape, thy love, thy wit,
Which like a usurer abound'st in all,
And usest none in that true use indeed
Which should bedeck thy shape, thy love, thy wit.
Thy noble shape is but a form of wax,   125
Digressing from the valour of a man;
Thy dear love sworn but hollow perjury,
Killing that love which thou hast vowed to cherish;
Thy wit, that ornament to shape and love,
Misshapen in the conduct of them both,   130
Like powder in a skilless soldier's flask,
Is set afire by thine own ignorance,
And thou dismembered with thine own defence.
What? Rouse thee, man! Thy Juliet is alive,

135 *lately*   recently.

    dead   wishing to die.

136 ***There***   because of that. Friar Lawrence repeats this several times, telling Romeo that he should count his blessings.

    happy   lucky, fortunate.

140 *light*   alight, fall.

144 *such*   people who behave like this.

145 *decreed*   arranged.

147 *the watch be set*   the guards take their places at the gates of the town. Friar Lawrence urges Romeo to leave Juliet's bedroom in good time.

150 *blaze*   announce.

153 *in lamentation*   wailing with grief.

156 *apt unto*   feel like doing.

161 *chide*   tell me off.

For whose dear sake thou wast but lately dead,   135
There art thou happy. Tybalt would kill thee,
But thou slew'st Tybalt; there art thou happy.
The law that threatened death becomes thy friend,
And turns it to exile; there art thou happy too.
A pack of blessings light upon thy back;   140
Happiness courts thee in her best array,
But like a misbehaved and sullen wench
Thou frown'st upon thy fortune and thy love.
Take heed, take heed, for such die miserable.
Go, get thee to thy love, as was decreed;   145
Ascend her chamber; hence, and comfort her,
But look thou stay not till the watch be set,
For then thou can'st not pass to Mantua,
Where thou shalt live till we can find a time
To blaze your marriage, reconcile your friends,   150
Beg pardon of the Prince, and call thee back
With twenty hundred thousand times more joy
Than thou went'st forth in lamentation.
Go before, Nurse. Commend me to thy lady,
And bid her hasten all the house to bed,   155
Which heavy sorrow makes them apt unto.
Romeo is coming.

NURSE

O Lord, I could have stayed here all the night
To hear good counsel. O what learning is!
My lord, I'll tell my lady you will come.   160

ROMEO

Do so, and bid my sweet prepare to chide.

NURSE

Here, sir, a ring she bid me give you, sir.
Hie you, make haste, for it grows very late.

164 *comfort* happiness.

165 *And here...state* follow these instructions if you wish to be happy.

168 *Sojourn* stay a while.

169 *signify* indicate, show.

170 *hap* event, piece of news.

to you in your interests.

172–3 *But that...thee* I would be sad to leave you, except that I am going to where I will be even happier.

1 *fallen out* occurred.

2 *move* persuade (to marry).

3 *Look you* understand that.

6 *promise* assure.

ROMEO
How well my comfort is revived by this.

FRIAR LAWRENCE
Go hence; good night.

Exit NURSE

        And here stands all your state: 165
Either be gone before the watch be set,
Or by the break of day disguised from hence.
Sojourn in Mantua. I'll find out your man,
And he shall signify from time to time
Every good hap to you that chances here.   170
Give me thy hand. 'T is late; farewell, good night.

ROMEO
But that a joy past joy calls out on me,
It were a grief so brief to part with thee.
Farewell.

Exeunt

Scene four

Capulet's house.

Enter CAPULET, LADY CAPULET, *and* PARIS.

CAPULET
Things have fallen out, sir, so unluckily
That we have had no time to move our daughter.
Look you, she loved her kinsman Tybalt dearly,
And so did I. Well, we were born to die.
'T is very late; she'll not come down tonight.   5
I promise you, but for your company,
I would have been a-bed an hour ago.

8 *afford*   give.

10 *know her mind*   find out her views.

11 *mewed up to*   shut away with. (Unknown to her parents, she is, of course, with Romeo).

12 *desperate tender*   daring offer.

13 *ruled*   advised, commanded.

16 *my son*   not literally, but Capulet is fairly confident that he will soon be his son-in-law.

17 *mark you me*   believe me.

23 *keep no great ado*   won't make a great fuss.

24 *so late*   so recently.

25 *held him carelessly*   did not care about him.

26 *revel much*   enjoy ourselves too much, have a big celebration.

PARIS

These times of woe afford no time to woo.
Madam, good night; commend me to your
    daughter.

LADY CAPULET

I will, and know her mind early to-morrow;   10
To-night she's mewed up to her heaviness.

CAPULET *calls back* PARIS *who is leaving.*

CAPULET

Sir Paris! I will make a desperate tender
Of my child's love. I think she will be ruled
In all respects by me: nay, more, I doubt it not.
Wife, go you to her ere you go to bed;   15
Acquaint her here of my son Paris' love,
And bid her, mark you me, on Wednesday next –
But soft, what day is this?

PARIS

                  Monday, my lord.

CAPULET

Monday, ah ha; well, Wednesday is too soon;
-O' Thursday let it be. O' Thursday, tell her,   20
She shall married to this noble earl.
Will you be ready? Do you like this haste?
We'll keep no great ado; a friend or two;
For hark you, Tybalt being slain so late,
It may be thought we held him carelessly,   25
Being our kinsman, if we revel much.
Therefore we'll have some half a dozen friends,
And there an end. (*To* PARIS) But what say you to
    Thursday?

29 *would* wish.

32 *against* for, in anticipation of.

34 *Afore me* My, my! – a mild swear word.

35 *by and by* soon.

2 *lark* bird that sings at daybreak. Juliet does not want the morning to come yet.

7 *envious* jealous.

8 *severing* breaking up. This also reflects the fact that the lovers will soon be parted.

9 *Night's candles* the stars.

   jocund joyful.

PARIS
    My lord, I would that Thursday were to-morrow.

CAPULET
    Well, get you gone; o' Thursday be it then.   30
    (*To his wife*) Go you to Juliet ere you go to bed;
    Prepare her, wife, against this wedding day.
    Farewell, my lord. (*To his Servant*) Light to my
       chamber, ho!
    Afore me, 't is so very late that we
    May call it early by and by. Good night.   35

                                       Exeunt

Scene five

Juliet's bedroom.

ROMEO *and* JULIET *stand at the window.*

JULIET
    Wilt thou be gone? It is not yet near day.
    It was the nightingale, and not the lark,
    That pierced the fearful hollow of thine ear.
    Nightly she sings on yond pomegranate tree.
    Believe me, love, it was the nightingale.   5

ROMEO
    It was the lark, the herald of the morn,
    No nightingale. Look, love, what envious streaks
    Do lace the severing clouds in yonder east.
    Night's candles are burnt out, and jocund day
    Stands tiptoe on the misty mountain tops.   10
    I must be gone and live, or stay and die.

13 *exhales*   breathes out, throws out.

17 *ta'en*   caught (taken).

18 *so thou...so*   if you are too.

20 *the pale reflex of Cynthia's brow*   a pale reflection of the moon (Cynthia was thought to be the goddess of the moon).

22 *vaulty*   vaulted, arched.

23 *care*   wish.

28 *sharps*   musical notes.

29 *division*   melody (but remember that Romeo and Juliet are about to part and this is a pun).

31 *Some say...eyes*   this refers to a belief that the lark and the toad swapped eyes as the toad had beautiful eyes in an ugly body.

32 *would*   wish.

33 *arm from arm*   from each other's arms.

   affray   frighten.

34 *hunt's up*   a hunting call, which got the huntsman out of bed early in the day.

JULIET

    Yond light is not daylight; I know it, I.
    It is some meteor that the sun exhales
    To be to thee this night a torchbearer
    And light thee on thy way to Mantua.   15
    Therefore stay yet; thou need'st not to be gone.

ROMEO

    Let me be ta'en, let me be put to death:
    I am content, so thou wilt have it so.
    I'll say yon grey is not the morning's eye,
    'T is but the pale reflex of Cynthia's brow;   20
    Nor that is not the lark whose notes do beat
    The vaulty heaven so high above our heads.
    I have more care to stay than will to go.
    Come, death, and welcome! Juliet wills it so.
    How is 't, my soul? Let's talk; it is not day.   25

JULIET

    It is, it is! Hie hence, be gone, away!
    It is the lark that sings so out of tune,
    Straining harsh discords and unpleasing sharps.
    Some say the lark makes sweet division:
    This doth not so, for she divideth us.   30
    Some say the lark and loathèd toad changed eyes;
    O now I would they had changed voices too,
    Since arm from arm that voice doth us affray,
    Hunting thee hence with hunt's-up to the day.
    O now be gone; more light and light grows.   35

ROMEO

    More light and light, more dark and dark our woes.

Enter NURSE, *in a hurry*.

NURSE

    Madam!

40 *look about*   beware.

41 *life*   Romeo is Juliet's life.

44 *in*   on.

46 *much in years*   old.

47 *ere*   before.

52 *discourses*   conversations.

53 *ill-divining*   pessimistic.

54 *low*   Juliet is looking down on Romeo who has descended the ladder.

JULIET

  Nurse?

NURSE

  Your lady mother is coming to your chamber.
  The day is broke; be wary, look about.   40

                       Exit NURSE

JULIET

  Then, window, let day in, and let life out.

ROMEO

  Farewell, farewell. One kiss and I'll descend.

                   He descends the ladder

JULIET

  Art thou gone so, love, lord, ay husband, friend?
  I must hear from thee every day in the hour,
  For in a minute there are many days.   45
  O, by this count I shall be much in years
  Ere I again behold my Romeo.

ROMEO

  (*From the garden below*) Farewell. I will omit no
    opportunity
  That may convey my greetings, love, to thee.

JULIET

  O, think'st thou we shall ever meet again?   50

ROMEO

  I doubt it not; and all these woes shall serve
  For sweet discourses in our time to come.

JULIET

  O God, I have an ill-divining soul!
  Methinks I see thee, now thou art so low,

58 *Dry*   parched, thirsty.
59 *fickle*   unfaithful, undependable.
60 *dost thou*   what do you want.
66 *procures*   brings.
67 *how now*   how are you?

As one dead in the bottom of a tomb; 55
Either my eyesight fails, or thou look'st pale.

ROMEO

And trust me, love, in my eye so do you.
Dry sorrow drinks our blood. Adieu, adieu.

Exit ROMEO

JULIET

O Fortune, Fortune, all men call thee fickle;
If thou art fickle, what dost thou with him 60
That is renowned for faith? Be fickle, Fortune,
For then I hope thou wilt not keep him long,
But send him back.

LADY CAPULET

(*Outside* JULIET's *door*) Ho, daughter, are you up?

JULIET

Who is 't that calls? It is my lady mother.
Is she not down so late, or up so early? 65
What unaccustomed cause procures her hither?

Enter LADY CAPULET.

LADY CAPULET

Why, how now, Juliet?

JULIET

Madam, I am not well.

LADY CAPULET

Evermore weeping for your cousin's death?
What, wilt thou wash him from his grave with
tears?
And if thou could'st, thou could'st not make him
live; 70

72 *want of wit*   lack of intelligence.
73 *feeling*   strongly felt.
80 *asunder*   apart.
85 *venge*   get revenge for.

Therefore have done: some grief shows much of
  love,
But much of grief shows still some want of wit.

JULIET
Yet let me weep for such a feeling loss.

LADY CAPULET
So shall you feel the loss, but not the friend
Which you weep for.

JULIET
                              Feeling so the loss,   75
I cannot choose but ever weep the friend.

LADY CAPULET
Well, girl, thou weep'st not so much for his death
As that the villain lives which slaughtered him.

JULIET
What villain, madam?

LADY CAPULET
                              That same villain, Romeo.

JULIET
(*Aside*) Villain and he be many miles asunder. –   80
(*To her mother*) God pardon him; I do, with all my
  heart;
And yet no man like he doth grieve my heart.

LADY CAPULET
That is because the traitor murderer lives.

JULIET
Ay, madam, from the reach of these my hands.
Would none but I might venge my cousin's death!   85

88 *runagate* fugitive.

89 *unaccustomed dram* strange drink, in other words, poison.

90 *keep Tybalt company* in death, or in the tomb.

93 *dead* Juliet is using this word to describe her 'poor heart', while her mother thinks she is referring to Romeo. Juliet is being ambiguous throughout this conversation with her mother.

94 *vexed* upset.

96 *temper* mix or weaken.

98 *sleep* Juliet intends a double meaning: sleep peacefully or die.

abhors hates.

100 *wreak* avenge or consummate.

102 *the means* the method, the way (to mix the poison).

104 *needy* sorrowful, when we are in need of cheering up.

106 *careful* caring, loving.

107 *heaviness* sadness.

108 *sudden* unexpected.

LADY CAPULET

    We will have vengeance for it, fear thou not.
    Then weep no more. I'll send to one in Mantua,
    Where that same banished runagate doth live,
    Shall give him such an unaccustomed dram
    That he shall soon keep Tybalt company;   90
    And then I hope thou wilt be satisfied.

JULIET

    Indeed, I never shall be satisfied
    With Romeo till I behold him; dead
    Is my poor heart, so for a kinsman vexed.
    Madam, if you could find out but a man   95
    To bear a poison, I would temper it
    That Romeo should upon receipt thereof
    Soon sleep in quiet. O how my heart abhors
    To hear him named and cannot come to him
    To wreak the love I bore my cousin   100
    Upon his body that hath slaughtered him.

LADY CAPULET

    Find thou the means, and I'll find such a man.
    But now I'll tell thee joyful tidings, girl.

JULIET

    And joy comes well in such a needy time.
    What are they, beseech your ladyship?   105

LADY CAPULET

    Well, well, thou hast a careful father, child;
    One who, to put thee from thy heaviness,
    Hath sorted out a sudden day of joy
    That thou expects not, nor I looked not for.

JULIET

    Madam, in happy time! What day is that?   110

114 *happily* fortunately.

117 *I wonder at* I am astonished by.

118 *should be* would like to be.

124 *at your hands* from you.

126 *sunset* death.

127 *rains downright* pours with rain (i.e. Juliet's tears).

128 *conduit* fountain, channel.

130 *counterfeits* looks like.

bark ship.

135 *overset* capsize.

137 *our decree* our decision.

LADY CAPULET

Marry, my child, early next Thursday morn,
The gallant, young, and noble gentleman,
The County Paris, at Saint Peter's Church,
Shall happily make thee there a joyful bride.

JULIET

Now, by Saint Peter's Church, and Peter too,   115
He shall not make me there a joyful bride.
I wonder at this haste, that I must wed
Ere he that should be my husband comes to woo.
I pray you tell my lord and father, madam,
I will not marry yet; and when I do, I swear   120
It shall be Romeo, whom you know I hate,
Rather than Paris. These are news indeed!

LADY CAPULET

Here comes your father; tell him so yourself,
And see how he will take it at your hands.

Enter CAPULET *and* NURSE.

CAPULET

When the sun sets, the earth doth drizzle dew;   125
But for the sunset of my brother's son
It rains downright.
How now, a conduit, girl? What, still in tears?
Evermore showering? In one little body
Thou counterfeits a bark, a sea, a wind;   130
For still thy eyes, which I may call the sea,
Do ebb and flow with tears; the bark thy body is,
Sailing in this salt flood; the winds thy sighs,
Who raging with thy tears, and they with them,
Without a sudden calm will overset   135
Thy tempest-tossèd body. How now, wife?
Have you delivered to her our decree?

213

138 *she will none*   she says she will not consider it.

140 *Soft, take me with you*   wait a moment, tell me again.

142 *proud*   satisfied.

    count her blest   count her blessings.

143 *wrought*   arranged for.

144 *bride*   groom (the word bride could, in Elizabethan times, be used for either sex).

147 *hate that is meant love*   the dreadful thing that you have done because you love me.

148 *chop-logic*   conundrums, playing with words.

150 *mistress minion*   rude young hussy.

152 *fettle your fine joints*   get your body ready (he is using the language usually used for horses, which may make us think that he treats Juliet here as he might treat his livestock).

154 *on a hurdle*   wooden cart or frame, usually used to take traitors to their place of execution.

155 *green-sickness carrion*   pale corpse (green-sickness was the name for anaemia).

    baggage   worthless woman.

156 *tallow-face*   pale-faced wretch (tallow was used for making candles).

LADY CAPULET

Ay, sir, but she will none, she gives you thanks.
I would the fool were married to her grave!

CAPULET

Soft, take me with you, take me with you, wife.   140
How will she none? Doth she not give us thanks?
Is she not proud? Doth she not count her blest,
Unworthy as she is, that we have wrought
So worthy a gentleman to be her bride?

JULIET

Not proud you have, but thankful that you have.   145
Proud can I never be of what I hate,
But thankful even for hate that is meant love.

CAPULET

How, how! how, how, chop-logic! What is this?
"Proud", and "I thank you", and "I thank you
    not",
And yet "Not proud", mistress minion you?   150
Thank me no thankings, nor proud me no prouds,
But fettle your fine joints 'gainst Thursday next,
To go with Paris to Saint Peter's Church,
Or I will drag thee on a hurdle thither.
Out, you green-sickness carrion! out, you baggage! 155
You tallow-face.

LADY CAPULET

(*To her husband*) Fie, fie! What, are you mad?

JULIET

Good father, I beseech you on my knees,
Hear me with patience but to speak a word.

CAPULET

Hang thee, young baggage! disobedient wretch!

163 *My fingers itch*   because I would like to slap you.

167 *Out on her, hilding!*   away with her, the contemptible beast.

168 *rate*   scold.

170 *Good Prudence*   not the Nurse's name, but said sarcastically, along the lines of Lady Wisdom.

Smatter   chatter idly.

171 *O God gi' good e'en*   good evening, but he is being dismissive and sarcastic.

173 *gravity*   serious words.

gossip's bowl   when you are drinking and nattering with your friends.

174 *hot*   angry.

175 *God's bread*   by the Communion bread (a strong swear word).

177 *still my care has been*   I have always been concerned.

I tell thee what: get thee to church o' Thursday,   160
Or never after look me in the face.
Speak not, reply not, do not answer me.
My fingers itch. Wife, we scarce thought us blest
That God had lent us but this only child,
But now I see this one is one too much,   165
And that we have a curse in having her.
Out on her, hilding!

NURSE

               God in heaven bless her!
You are to blame, my lord, to rate her so.

CAPULET

And why, my Lady Wisdom? Hold your tongue,
Good Prudence. Smatter with your gossips, go.   170

NURSE

I speak no treason.

CAPULET

              O God gi' good e'en!

NURSE

May not one speak?

CAPULET

              Peace, you mumbling fool!
Utter your gravity o'er a gossip's bowl,
For here we need it not.

LADY CAPULET

              You are too hot.

CAPULET

God's bread! it makes me mad.   175
Day, night, hour, tide, time, work, play,
Alone, in company, still my care hath been

178 *matched* married.

180 *fair demesnes* wealthy estates.

181 *parts* qualities.

182 *Proportioned* made.

183 *puling* whinging.

184 *mammet* puppet.

in her fortune's tender when she is lucky enough to be made such an offer.

187 *But and you will not* but if you will not.

188 *Graze* eat.

house live in the same house.

189 *I do not use to jest* I do not usually make jokes.

190 *advise* think about it carefully.

191 *And* if.

194 *Nor what...good* Capulet is threatening to disinherit her.

195 *Trust...forsworn* trust me and think about it because I will not be disobeyed.

202 *speak a word* put in a good word for you to your father.

To have her matched; and having now provided
A gentleman of noble parentage,
Of fair demesnes, youthful and nobly trained,⠀⠀⠀180
Stuffed, as they say, with honourable parts,
Proportioned as one's thought would wish a man,
And then to have a wretched puling fool,
A whining mammet, in her fortune's tender,
To answer "I'll not wed, I cannot love,⠀⠀⠀185
I am too young, I pray you pardon me"!
But and you will not wed I'll pardon you:
Graze where you will, you shall not house with me.
Look to 't, think on 't; I do not use to jest.
Thursday is near; lay hand on heart, advise.⠀⠀⠀190
And you be mine, I'll give you to my friend:
And you be not, hang, beg, starve, die in the streets,
For, by my soul, I'll ne'er acknowledge thee,
Nor what is mine shall never do thee good.
Trust to 't, bethink you; I'll not be forsworn.⠀⠀⠀195

Exit CAPULET

JULIET
⠀⠀⠀Is there no pity sitting in the clouds
⠀⠀⠀That sees into the bottom of my grief?
⠀⠀⠀O sweet my mother, cast me not away!
⠀⠀⠀Delay this marriage for a month, a week;
⠀⠀⠀Or, if you do not, make the bridal bed⠀⠀⠀200
⠀⠀⠀In that dim monument where Tybalt lies.

LADY CAPULET
⠀⠀⠀Talk not to me, for I'll not speak a word.
⠀⠀⠀Do as thou wilt, for I have done with thee.

Exit LADY CAPULET

JULIET
⠀⠀⠀O God! O Nurse, how shall this be prevented?

219

205–8 *my faith...leaving earth*   God has heard my marriage vows and I cannot take them again unless my husband allows me to by dying.

209 *practise stratagems*   plot.

213–4 *all the world...you*   I'd bet the world that he never comes back to claim you as his wife.

219 *dishclout*   a dishcloth.

221 *Beshrew my very heart*   may I be cursed if I am wrong.

225 *you no use of him*   without the benefit of him as a husband.

226 *from thy heart*   your true feelings.

228 *Amen*   so be it, I agree.

My husband is on earth, my faith in heaven; 205
How shall that faith return again to earth,
Unless that husband send it me from heaven
By leaving earth? Comfort me, counsel me.
Alack, alack, that heaven should practise stratagems
Upon so soft a subject as myself? 210
What say'st thou? Hast thou not a word of joy?
Some comfort, Nurse.

NURSE

     Faith, here it is: Romeo
Is banishèd; and all the world to nothing
That he dares ne'er come back to challenge you;
Or if he do, it needs must be by stealth. 215
Then since the case so stands as now it doth,
I think it best you married with the County.
O, he's a lovely gentleman!
Romeo's dishclout to him. An eagle, madam,
Hath not so green, so quick, so fair an eye 220
As Paris hath. Beshrew my very heart,
I think you are happy in this second match,
For it excels your first; or if it did not,
Your first is dead, or 't were as good he were,
As living here, and you no use of him. 225

JULIET
Speak'st thou from thy heart?

NURSE
And from my soul too; else beshrew them both.

JULIET
Amen!

NURSE
 What?

235 *Ancient damnation* damned old hag.

236 *sin* sinful.

wish me thus forsworn want me to go back on my marriage vows (by marrying Paris).

237 *dispraise* speak ill of.

240 *twain* separated. Juliet is no longer going to turn to the Nurse for support and advice.

242 *myself have power to die* I can take my life into my own hands.

JULIET

Well, thou hast comforted me marvellous much.   230
Go in and tell my lady I am gone,
Having displeased my father, to Lawrence' cell
To make confession and to be absolved.

NURSE

Marry, I will; and this is wisely done.

Exit NURSE

JULIET

Ancient damnation! O most wicked fiend!   235
Is it more sin to wish me thus forsworn,
Or to dispraise my lord with that same tongue
Which she hath praised him with above compare
So many thousand times? Go, counsellor,
Thou and my bosom henceforth shall be twain.   240
I'll to the Friar, to know his remedy.
If all else fail, myself have power to die.

Exit JULIET

Act 4: summary

When Juliet arrives at the Friar's cell she finds that Paris is there making the wedding arrangements. She has to be on her guard until she can speak to the Friar alone. He gives her a sleeping potion to enable her to fake her death so that she may avoid the wedding. The Friar says he will write to Romeo to tell him of their plan and that he will send for him to collect Juliet in two nights' time.

Lord Capulet has already set the preparations for the wedding feast in motion and the house is a flurry of activity. When Juliet returns, apparently ready to do as her father wishes, he is so overjoyed he brings the wedding forward to Wednesday (the next day). Alone and afraid, Juliet knows she must now take the sleeping draught in spite of what might befall.

The household is busy all night long and early on Wednesday morning Paris arrives with a procession of musicians to lead Juliet to church. It is only then that the Nurse discovers the seemingly lifeless body of Juliet. Everyone is grief-stricken and Friar Lawrence encourages them to prepare her for burial in the family vault as quickly as possible, as he knows the effects of the potion will soon wear off.

(Opposite) Dilys Hamlett as the Nurse and Sarah Woodward as Juliet: the New Shakespeare Company at the Open Air Theatre, Regent's Park, 1986 (© John Timbers Studio).

2 *father* Capulet will become Paris' father-in-law when he and Juliet are married.

3 *nothing slow to slack his haste* I am not going to be slow, because that would slow Capulet down too.

5 *Uneven is the course* this is not the usual way of doing things.

8 *Venus* goddess of love; love does not go well with sadness.

9 *counts* thinks.

10 *give . . . so much sway* gives in to her grief.

12 *inundation* deluge, flood.

13 *minded by herself alone* having spent too much time brooding alone.

14 *society* company.

Act Four

Scene one

Friar Lawrence's cell.

Enter FRIAR LAWRENCE *and* PARIS.

FRIAR LAWRENCE
On Thursday, sir? The time is very short.

PARIS
My father Capulet will have it so,
And I am nothing slow to slack his haste.

FRIAR LAWRENCE
You say you do not know the lady's mind?
Uneven is the course; I like it not.   5

PARIS
Immoderately she weeps for Tybalt's death,
And therefore have I little talked of love,
For Venus smiles not in a house of tears.
Now, sir, her father counts it dangerous
That she do give her sorrow so much sway,   10
And in his wisdom hastes our marriage,
To stop the inundation of her tears,
Which, too much minded by herself alone,
May be put from her by society.
Now do you know the reason of this haste.   15

FRIAR LAWRENCE
(*Aside*) I would I knew not why it should be slowed. –
Look, sir, here comes the lady toward my cell.

20 *must be*   will be (because that is the day of their wedding). Paris is displaying over-confidence which in the circumstances is ironic.

21 *a certain text*   true enough.

27 *price*   worth.

29 *abused*   harmed, spoiled.

Enter JULIET.

PARIS

Happily met, my lady and my wife!

JULIET

That may be, sir, when I may be a wife.

PARIS

That "may be" must be, love, on Thursday next.   20

JULIET

What must be shall be.

FRIAR LAWRENCE

That's a certain text.

PARIS

Come you to make confession to this father?

JULIET

To answer that, I should confess to you.

PARIS

Do not deny to him that you love me.

JULIET

I will confess to you that I love him.   25

PARIS

So will ye, I am sure, that you love me.

JULIET

If I do so, it will be of more price,
Being spoke behind your back, than to your face.

PARIS

Poor soul, thy face is much abused with tears.

31 *spite* spitefulness.

34 *to my face* honestly and referring to my own face.

35 *mine* as soon as they are married Juliet will belong to Paris, so he says presumptuously that her face belongs to him.

39 *pensive* thoughtful.

40 *entreat* ask for.

41 *shield* forbid.

JULIET

The tears have got small victory by that,   30
For it was bad enough before their spite.

PARIS

Thou wrong'st it more than tears with that report.

JULIET

That is no slander, sir, which is a truth,
And what I spake, I spake it to my face.

PARIS

Thy face is mine, and thou hast slandered it.   35

JULIET

It may be so, for it is not mine own. –
Are you at leisure, holy Father, now,
Or shall I come to you at evening Mass?

FRIAR LAWRENCE

My leisure serves me, pensive daughter, now.
My lord, we must entreat the time alone.   40

PARIS

God shield I should disturb devotion.
Juliet, on Thursday early will I rouse ye;
Till then, adieu, and keep this holy kiss.

He kisses her and leaves

JULIET

O shut the door, and when thou hast done so,
Come weep with me, past hope, past care, past
    help.   45

FRIAR LAWRENCE

O Juliet, I already know thy grief;

47 *It strains . . . wits*   I cannot for the life of me think of a way to stop this (Juliet's anguish).

48 *prorogue*   put off.

53 *resolution*   resolve, determination.

54 *presently*   now.

55 *thou our hands*   you married us.

56 *ere*   before.

57 *the label to another deed*   the seal on another marriage contract.

59 *this*   this knife.

60 *out of*   on account of, because of.

time   life.

61 *present*   immediate.

62 *'Twixt my extremes and me*   between me and the situation I am in.

63 *playing the umpire*   be the one to make the decision, as in a game.

arbitrating   judging.

64 *commission*   authority.

art   skill.

65 *issue*   ending.

68 *Hold*   wait.

69 *craves as . . . execution*   needs you to act just as desperately (as you are talking of doing now).

74 *to chide away*   to avoid.

75 *cop'st with*   prepares for, faces up to.

It strains me past the compass of my wits.
I hear thou must, and nothing may prorogue it,
On Thursday next be married to this County.

JULIET

Tell me not, Friar, that thou hearest of this,   50
Unless thou tell me how I may prevent it.
If in thy wisdom thou can'st give no help,
Do thou but call my resolution wise,
And with this knife I'll help it presently.
God joined my heart and Romeo's, thou our hands; 55
And ere this hand, by thee to Romeo's sealed,
Shall be the label to another deed,
Or my true heart with treacherous revolt
Turn to another, this shall slay them both.
Therefore, out of thy long-experienced time,   60
Give me some present counsel; or, behold,
'Twixt my extremes and me, this bloody knife
Shall play the umpire, arbitrating that
Which the commission of thy years and art
Could to no issue of true honour bring.   65
Be not so long to speak; I long to die
If what thou speak'st speak not of remedy.

FRIAR LAWRENCE

Hold, daughter: I do spy a kind of hope,
Which craves as desperate an execution
As that is desperate which we would prevent.   70
If, rather than to marry County Paris,
Thou hast the strength of will to slay thyself,
Then is it likely thou wilt undertake
A thing like death to chide away this shame,
That cop'st with death himself to scape from it;   75
And, if thou darest, I'll give thee remedy.

79 *thievish ways*   places where thieves are found.

80 *roaring bears*   this is a reference to bear-baiting, popular at the time.

81 *charnel house*   place where old bones were stored after they had been dug up to make way for new graves.

83 *reeky*   foul-smelling.

shanks   leg-bones.

chapless skulls   skulls with no jaws.

91 *look*   see, make sure.

93 *vial*   small bottle used for herbal remedies or poisons.

94 *distillèd liquor*   boiled down plant juices.

off   up.

95 *presently*   immediately.

96 *humour*   sensation.

97 *Shall keep . . . surcease*   her pulse will not continue at its normal rate but will seem to stop.

98 *testify*   show, prove.

100 *wanny*   pale; wan.

eye's windows   eyelids.

102 *deprived of supple government*   losing its ability to move.

104 *borrowed likeness*   false image.

JULIET

O bid me leap, rather than marry Paris,
From off the battlements of any tower,
Or walk in thievish ways, or bid me lurk
Where serpents are; chain me with roaring bears,   80
Or hide me nightly in a charnel house,
O'ercovered quite with dead men's rattling bones,
With reeky shanks and yellow chapless skulls;
Or bid me go into a new-made grave,
And hide me with a dead man in his shroud –   85
Things that, to hear them told, have made me
    tremble –
And I will do it without fear or doubt,
To live an unstained wife to my sweet love.

FRIAR LAWRENCE

Hold, then. Go home, be merry, give consent
To marry Paris. Wednesday is to-morrow: 90
To-morrow night look that thou lie alone;
Let not the Nurse lie with thee in thy chamber.
Take thou this vial, being then in bed,
And this distillèd liquor drink thou off,
When presently through all thy veins shall run   95
A cold and drowsy humour, for no pulse
Shall keep his native progress, but surcease;
No warmth, no breath, shall testify thou livest;
The roses in thy lips and cheeks shall fade
To wanny ashes, thy eyes' windows fall   100
Like death when he shuts up the day of life.
Each part, deprived of supple government,
Shall, stiff and stark and cold, appear like death,
And in this borrowed likeness of shrunk death
Thou shalt continue two and forty hours,   105
And then awake as from a pleasant sleep.

108 *art thou*   you are (but really you appear to be).

109 *as the manner of the country is*   as is the custom in this country.

110 *uncovered on the bier*   not in a coffin but carried on a bier, visible for all to see.

113 *against thou shalt wake*   ready for when you wake up.

114 *know our drift*   learn what we are up to.

119 *inconstant toy*   change of heart.

120 *Abate thy . . . acting of it*   stop you feeling brave enough to carry it out.

122 *prosperous*   successful.

125 *afford*   provide.

Now, when the bridegroom in the morning comes
To rouse thee from thy bed, there art thou dead.
Then, as the manner of our country is,
In thy best robes, uncovered on the bier,   110
Thou shalt be borne to that same ancient vault
Where all the kindred of the Capulets lie.
In the meantime, against thou shalt awake,
Shall Romeo by my letters know our drift,
And hither shall he come; and he and I   115
Will watch thy waking, and that very night
Shall Romeo bear thee hence to Mantua.
And this shall free thee from this present shame,
If no inconstant toy nor womanish fear
Abate thy valour in the acting it.   120

JULIET

Give me, give me! O tell not me of fear!

FRIAR LAWRENCE

Hold; get you gone. Be strong and prosperous
In this resolve. I'll send a friar with speed
To Mantua, with my letters to thy lord.

JULIET

Love give me strength! and strength shall help
    afford.   125
Farewell, dear Father.

Exeunt

1 *So* as.
2 *cunning* clever.
3 *ill* bad.
  try test.
10 *much unfurnished* nowhere near ready.
12 *forsooth* indeed.

Scene two

Capulet's house.

Enter CAPULET, LADY CAPULET, NURSE *and* SERVANTS.

CAPULET
  (*Giving a paper to a* SERVANT) So many guests invite
    as here are writ.

Exit SERVANT

  (*To another* SERVANT) Sirrah, go hire me twenty cun-
    ning cooks.

SERVANT
  You shall have none ill, sir, for I'll try if they can
    lick their fingers.

CAPULET
  How can'st thou try them so?   5

SERVANT
  Marry, sir, 't is an ill cook that cannot lick his own
    fingers. Therefore he that cannot lick his own
    fingers goes not with me.

CAPULET
  Go, be gone.

Exit SERVANT

  We shall be much unfurnished for this time.   10
  What, is my daughter gone to Friar Lawrence?

NURSE
  Ay, forsooth.

14 *A peevish, self-willed harlotry it is*   she is a stubborn and determined little madam.

15 *shrift*   see note to Act 2, scene 3, line 174.

16 *gadding*   running about.

18 *disobedient opposition*   going against (you).

19 *behests*   wishes.

   enjoined   instructed.

20 *fall prostrate*   fall on my knees.

24 *knot knit up*   marriage tied up (thus to 'tie the knot').

26 *becomèd*   appropriate.

27 *Not o'erstepping . . . modesty*   without being too forward.

32 *bound to*   indebted.

CAPULET

Well, he may chance to do some good on her.
A peevish, self-willed harlotry it is.

Enter JULIET.

NURSE

See where she comes from shrift with merry look.   15

CAPULET

How now, my headstrong? Where have you been
gadding?

JULIET

Where I have learnt me to repent the sin
Of disobedient opposition
To you and your behests, and am enjoined
By holy Lawrence to fall prostrate here   20
To beg your pardon. (*She kneels*) Pardon, I beseech
you.
Henceforward I am ever ruled by you.

CAPULET

Send for the County; go, tell him of this.
I'll have this knot knit up to-morrow morning.

JULIET

I met the youthful lord at Lawrence' cell,   25
And gave him what becomèd love I might,
Not stepping o'er the bounds of modesty.

CAPULET

Why, I am glad on 't; this is well. Stand up.
This is as 't should be. Let me see the County:
Ay, marry, go, I say, and fetch him hither.   30
Now, afore God, this reverend holy Friar –
All our whole city is much bound to him.

33 *closet*   room.

34 *needful*   necessary.

35 *to furnish me*   for me to put on.

38 *We shall . . . provision*   we will not have all the things we need for the wedding.

39 *Tush*   nonsense.

   stir about   busy myself.

40 *warrant*   promise.

41 *deck*   dress.

44 *They are all forth*   the servants are all about their business.

46 *Against*   for.

47 *reclaimed*   brought to her senses.

JULIET

  Nurse, will you go with me into my closet
  To help me sort such needful ornaments
  As you think fit to furnish me to-morrow?   35

LADY CAPULET

  No, not till Thursday; there is time enough.

CAPULET

  Go, Nurse, go with her. We'll to church to-morrow.

                 Exeunt JULIET *and* NURSE

LADY CAPULET

  We shall be short in our provision.
  'T is now near night.

CAPULET

                Tush, I will stir about,
  And all things shall be well, I warrant thee, wife.   40
  Go thou to Juliet: help to deck up her.
  I'll not to bed to-night. Let me alone;
  I'll play the housewife for this once. (*He calls the
    Servants*) What ho!
  They are all forth. Well, I will walk myself
  To County Paris, to prepare up him   45
  Against to-morrow. My heart is wondrous light
  Since this same wayward girl is so reclaimed.

          Exeunt CAPULET *and* LADY CAPULET

1 *attires* clothes.

2 *orisons* prayers.

4 *state* predicament.

5 *cross* wrong.

7 *culled* got together.

8 *behoveful* suitable.

state ceremony.

12 *sudden* rushed.

Scene three

Juliet's bedroom.

Enter JULIET *and* NURSE.

JULIET
    Ay, those attires are best; but, gentle Nurse,
    I pray thee leave me to myself to-night,
    For I have need of many orisons
    To move the heavens to smile upon my state,
    Which well thou knowest is cross and full of sin.   5

Enter LADY CAPULET.

LADY CAPULET
    What, are you busy, ho? Need you my help?

JULIET
    No, madam; we have culled such necessaries
    As are behoveful for our state to-morrow:
    So please you, let me now be left alone,
    And let the Nurse this night sit up with you,   10
    For I am sure you have your hands full all
    In this so sudden business.

LADY CAPULET
                   Good night.
    Get thee to bed and rest, for thou hast need.

                  Exeunt LADY CAPULET *and* NURSE

JULIET
    Farewell. – God knows when we shall meet again.
    I have a faint cold fear thrills through my veins,   15
    That almost freezes up the heat of life.
    I'll call them back again to comfort me.
    (*She calls*) Nurse! – What should she do here?

25 *ministered*   given to me.

29 *tried*   shown to be.

32 *redeem*   save.

34 *healthsome*   wholesome, fresh.

35 *strangled*   stifled.

37 *horrible conceit*   terrible thought.

42 *green in earth*   not long buried.

44 *resort*   meet.

47 *mandrakes*   the mandrake root resembled a human body. It was believed that these plants would scream if they were pulled up by the roots, sending the person who did it mad.

49 *distraught*   driven mad.

50 *Environed*   surrounded.

My dismal scene I needs must act alone.
Come, vial. 20
What if this mixture do not work at all?
Shall I be married then to-morrow morning?
No, no. This shall forbid it. (*She lays down her knife*)
   Lie thou there.
What if it be a poison which the Friar
Subtly hath ministered to have me dead, 25
Lest in this marriage he should be dishonoured
Because he married me before to Romeo?
I fear it is; and yet methinks it should not,
For he hath still been tried a holy man.
How if, when I am laid into the tomb, 30
I wake before the time that Romeo
Come to redeem me? There's a fearful point!
Shall I not then be stifled in the vault,
To whose foul mouth no healthsome air breathes in,
And there die strangled ere my Romeo comes? 35
Or, if I live, is it not very like
The horrible conceit of death and night,
Together with the terror of the place –
As in a vault, an ancient receptacle,
Where, for this many hundred years, the bones 40
Of all my buried ancestors are packed;
Where bloody Tybalt yet but green in earth,
Lies festering in his shroud; where, as they say,
At some hours in the night spirits resort –
Alack, alack! is it not like that I, 45
So early waking, what with loathsome smells
And shrieks like mandrakes torn out of the earth,
That living mortals, hearing them run mad –
O, if I walk, shall I not be distraught,
Environed with all these hideous fears, 50
And madly play with my forefathers' joints,

53 *rage*   mad fit.

56 *spit*   ran a sword through his body like an animal on a roasting spit.

57 *Stay*   stop.

2 *pastry*   room where pastry was made, kitchen.

3 *stir*   come quickly.

4 *curfew*   bells were often rung in towns and cities to warn people to put out their hearth fires for the night (because of the risk of fire). Usually the bells rang in the late evening and early morning, so it is not certain what bell Capulet is actually referring to here, unless it is the morning one.

5 *baked meats*   meat pies.

6 *cot-quean*   meddling man. She is saying that Capulet has no business occupying himself with housewifely matters.

8 *watching*   vigil, staying up late.

And pluck the mangled Tybalt from his shroud,
And in this rage, with some great kinsman's bone,
As with a club, dash out my desperate brains?
O look! methinks I see my cousin's ghost,   55
Seeking out Romeo that did spit his body
Upon a rapier's point. Stay, Tybalt, stay!
Romeo, I come! this do I drink to thee.

She falls on her bed.

Scene four

The hall in Capulet's house.

Enter LADY CAPULET *and* NURSE *who carries herbs.*

LADY CAPULET
    Hold, take these keys and fetch more spices, Nurse.

NURSE
    They call for dates and quinces in the pastry.

Enter CAPULET.

CAPULET
    Come, stir, stir, stir! The second cock hath crowed,
    The curfew bell hath rung, 't is three o'clock.
    Look to the baked meats, good Angelica;   5
    Spare not for cost.

NURSE
              Go, ye cot-quean, go.
    Get you to bed. Faith, you'll be sick to-morrow
    For this night's watching.

9 *not a whit*   not at all.

11 *mouse-hunt*   womaniser, chaser of women.

12 *watch*   prevent.

13 *jealous hood*   jealous woman.

17 *I have a head*   I have enough sense, I know how to.

19 *Mass*   by the Mass – a swear word.

    whoreson   rogue (son of a whore).

20 *loggerhead*   blockhead, idiot (a pun on logs).

21 *straight*   soon, at any moment.

24 *trim her up*   get her ready.

CAPULET

No, not a whit. What! I have watched ere now
All night for lesser cause and ne'er been sick.   10

LADY CAPULET

Ay, you have been a mouse-hunt in your time,
But I will watch you from such watching now.

Exeunt LADY CAPULET *and* NURSE

CAPULET

A jealous hood, a jealous hood!

Enter SERVANTS *with spits, logs, and baskets.*

Now, fellow, what is there?

SERVANT

Things for the cook, sir, but I know not what.

CAPULET

Make haste, make haste, sirrah. Fetch drier logs.   15
Call Peter; he will show thee where they are.

SERVANT

I have a head, sir, that will find out logs.
And never trouble Peter for the matter.

CAPULET

Mass, and well said; a merry whoreson, ha!
Thou shalt be loggerhead. – Good faith, 't is day!   20
The County will be here with music straight,
For so he said he would. (*Music sounds*) I hear him
near.
Nurse! Wife! What ho! What, Nurse, I say!

Enter NURSE.

Go waken Juliet; go, and trim her up.

1   *Fast*   sound asleep.

2   *slug-a-bed*   lazy-bones.

4   *pennyworths*   little portions, cat-naps.

6   *set up his rest*   set his mind on.

10   *take you*   find you, but also in the sexual sense.

11   *fright you up*   startle you into waking up.

12   *down*   lying down.

13   *I must needs*   I have to.

15   *well-a-day*   expression of despair.

I'll go and chat with Paris. Hie, make haste,   25
Make haste! The bridegroom he is come already.
Make haste, I say.

Exeunt all except NURSE

Scene five

Juliet's bedroom.

NURSE

(*Calling outside the bed-curtains*) Mistress! what,
   mistress! Fast, I warrant her, she.
Why, lamb! why, lady! Fie, you slug-a-bed!
Why, love, I say! madam! sweetheart! why, bride!
What, not a word? You take your pennyworths
   now;
Sleep for a week; for the next night, I warrant,   5
The County Paris hath set up his rest
That you shall rest but little. God forgive me!
Marry, and amen! How sound is she asleep!
I needs must wake her. Madam, madam, madam!
Ay, let the County take you in your bed;   10
He'll fright you up, i' faith. Will it not be?

She opens the bed-curtains.

What, dressed, and in your clothes, and down
   again?
I must needs wake you. Lady, lady, lady!
Alas, alas! Help, help! My lady's dead!
O well-a-day that ever I was born!   15
Some aqua-vitae, ho! My lord! my lady!

26 *settled* still, congealed.
28 *untimely* wrongly timed, tragically early.

Enter LADY CAPULET.

LADY CAPULET
  What noise is here?

NURSE
                    O lamentable day!

LADY CAPULET
  What is the matter?

NURSE
                    Look, look! O heavy day!

LADY CAPULET
  O me, O me! My child, my only life,
  Revive, look up, or I will die with thee!   20
  Help, help! Call help!

Enter CAPULET.

CAPULET
  For shame, bring Juliet forth; her lord is come.

NURSE
  She's dead, deceased; she's dead, alack the day!

LADY CAPULET
  Alack the day, she's dead, she's dead, she's dead!

CAPULET
  Ha, let me see her. Out, alas! she's cold;   25
  Her blood is settled, and her joints are stiff.
  Life and these lips have long been separated.
  Death lies on her like an untimely frost
  Upon the sweetest flower of all the field.

NURSE
  O lamentable day!

36 *Hath Death . . . wife* death has spent the night with your wife to be.

37 *defloweréd* violated, no longer a virgin.

40 *living* wealth and estate.

41 *thought* waited.

45 *In lasting . . . pilgrimage* during the endless toil of his journey through the ages.

46 *But one* (I had) only one.

47 *solace* find comfort.

48 *catched* torn, taken.

LADY CAPULET
> O woeful time!   30

CAPULET
Death, that hath ta'en her hence to make me wail,
Ties up my tongue and will not let me speak.

Enter FRIAR LAWRENCE *and* PARIS.

FRIAR LAWRENCE
Come, is the bride ready to go to church?

CAPULET
Ready to go, but never to return.
O son, the night before thy wedding day   35
Hath Death lain with thy wife. There she lies,
Flower as she was, deflowerèd by him.
Death is my son-in-law, Death is my heir;
My daughter he hath wedded. I will die
And leave him all. Life, living, all is Death's.   40

PARIS
Have I thought long to see this morning's face,
And doth it give me such a sight as this?

LADY CAPULET
Accursed, unhappy, wretched, hateful day!
Most miserable hour that e'er Time saw
In lasting labour of his pilgrimage.   45
But one poor one, one poor and loving child;
But one thing to rejoice and solace in,
And cruel Death hath catched it from my sight.

NURSE
O woe! O woeful, woeful, woeful day!
Most lamentable day, most woeful day   50
That ever, ever I did yet behold!

55 *Beguiled*   duped, misled.

   divorcèd   separated.

60 *Uncomfortable*   bringing discomfort or pain.

61 *solemnity*   wedding feast.

65–6 *Confusion's cure . . . confusions*   you will not make things any better by
   wailing over them.

67 *Had part in*   together created.

70 *eternal life*   life after death.

71 *her promotion*   making a better life for her.

72 *your heaven*   your own happiness (that Juliet should marry well).

76 *well*   in a happier state in heaven.

79 *rosemary*   herb that was used at both weddings and funerals to signify
   remembrance.

80 *corse*   dead body.

O day, O day, O day, O hateful day!
Never was seen so black a day as this.
O woeful day, O woeful day!

PARIS

Beguiled, divorcèd, wrongèd, spited, slain!   55
Most detestable Death, by thee beguiled;
By cruel, cruel thee quite overthrown!
O love! O life! Not life, but love in death!

CAPULET

Despised, distressed, hated, martyred, killed!
Uncomfortable Time, why cam'st thou now   60
To murder, murder our solemnity?
O child, O child! my soul, and not my child!
Dead art thou. Alack, my child is dead,
And with my child my joys are burièd.

FRIAR LAWRENCE

Peace, ho, for shame! Confusion's cure lives not   65
In these confusions. Heaven and yourself
Had part in this fair maid: now Heaven hath all,
And all the better is it for the maid.
Your part in her you could not keep from Death,
But heaven keeps his part in eternal life.   70
The most you sought was her promotion,
For 't was your heaven she should be advanced;
And weep ye now, seeing she is advanced
Above the clouds, as high as heaven itself?
O, in this love you love your child so ill   75
That you run mad, seeing that she is well.
She's not well married that lives married long,
But she's best married that dies married young.
Dry up your tears, and stick your rosemary
On this fair corse, and as the custom is,   80

82 *fond nature*   natural affection.

83 *nature's tears. . .merriment*   tears are uncontrolled (irrational) which our logical minds find laughable.

84 *ordainèd festival*   planned as part of the celebration.

85 *office*   purpose.

86 *instruments*   musical instruments.

87 *cheer*   feast.

88 *dirges*   burial hymns.

94 *lour*   scowl.

    ill   misdeed.

95 *Move*   annoy.

    crossing   going against.

96 *put up*   put away.

99 *the case may be amended*   these things could be sorted out.

In all her best array bear her to church,
For though fond nature bids us all lament,
Yet nature's tears are reason's merriment.

CAPULET

All things that we ordainèd festival
Turn from their office to black funeral: 85
Our instruments to melancholy bells,
Our wedding cheer to a sad burial feast,
Our solemn hymns to sullen dirges change,
Our bridal flowers serve for a buried corse,
And all things change them to the contrary.   90

FRIAR LAWRENCE

Sir, go you in; and, madam, go with him;
And go, Sir Paris. Everyone prepare
To follow this fair corse unto her grave.
The heavens do lour upon you for some ill:
Move them no more by crossing their high will.   95

They place rosemary on JULIET'S *body and close the bed-
curtains.*

Exeunt all except NURSE

Enter MUSICIANS.

FIRST MUSICIAN

Faith, we may put up our pipes and be gone.

NURSE

Honest good fellows, ah, put up, put up,
For well you know this is a pitiful case.

FIRST MUSICIAN

Ay, by my troth, the case may be amended.

Exit NURSE

Enter PETER.

100 *Heart's ease*   popular song in Elizabethan time.

101 *and*   if.

105 *dump*   sad song.

110 *give it you*   settle up with you.

112 *the gleek*   scorn.

113 *the minstrel*   an insult for musicians to be referred to thus.

114 *serving-creature*   an even bigger insult than serving-man.

116 *pate*   head.

carry no crotchets   not put up with your little games.

117 *note*   understand.

PETER

Musicians, O musicians, "Heart's ease", "Heart's 100
ease"! O, and you will have me live, play "Heart's
ease".

FIRST MUSICIAN

Why "Heart's ease"?

PETER

O musicians, because my heart itself plays "My
heart is full". O play me some merry dump to 105
comfort me.

FIRST MUSICIAN

Not a dump, we. 'T is no time to play now.

PETER

You will not then?

FIRST MUSICIAN

No.

PETER

I will then give it you soundly.   110

FIRST MUSICIAN

What will you give us?

PETER

No money, on my faith, but the gleek. I will give
you the minstrel.

FIRST MUSICIAN

Then will I give you the serving-creature.

PETER

Then will I lay the serving-creature's dagger on 115
your pate. I will carry no crotchets. I'll re you,
I'll fa you. Do you note me?

118 *note us*   set us to music.

119 *put out your wit*   stop being so clever.

120 *have at*   challenge.

dry-beat   batter.

123–5 *When griping grief . . . sound*   the first few lines of a song called 'In Commendation of Music', by Richard Edwards, published in 1576.

124 *doleful dumps*   sad sorrows; see also note to line 105 on page 262.

127 *Catling*   lute string made of cat gut.

129 *Rebeck*   three-stringed fiddle.

130 *sound*   play.

132 *Soundpost*   violin peg.

134 *I cry you mercy*   I beg your pardon.

136 *have no gold for sounding*   get no money for playing.

FIRST MUSICIAN

And you re us and fa us, you note us.

SECOND MUSICIAN

Pray you, put up your dagger, and put out your wit.

PETER

Then have at you with my wit! I will dry-beat you 120
with an iron wit, and put up my iron dagger.
Answer me like men:
When griping grief the heart doth wound,
And doleful dumps the mind oppress,
Then music with her silver sound –   125
Why "silver sound"? Why "music with her silver
sound"? What say you, Simon Catling?

FIRST MUSICIAN

Marry, sir, because silver hath a sweet sound.

PETER

Pretty! What say you, Hugh Rebeck?

SECOND MUSICIAN

I say "silver sound" because musicians sound for 130
silver.

PETER

Pretty too! What say you, James Soundpost?

THIRD MUSICIAN

Faith, I know not what to say.

PETER

O, I cry you mercy! You are the singer. I will say for
you. It is "music with her silver sound" because 135
musicians have no gold for sounding.

138 *lend redress*   make up for it.
139 *pestilent knave*   awful rogue.
140 *Jack*   scoundrel
   tarry   stay behind.
141 *stay*   wait for.

Then music with her silver sound
With speedy help doth lend redress.

Exit PETER

FIRST MUSICIAN
What a pestilent knave is this same!

SECOND MUSICIAN
Hang him, Jack! Come, we'll in here, tarry for the 140
mourners, and stay dinner.

Exeunt

Act 5: summary

Balthasar, Romeo's servant, rushes to Mantua with news of Juliet's death. Romeo immediately decides to ride to Verona that night to be with her for the last time, and he purchases poison from an apothecary.

Meanwhile in Verona, Friar John reports to Lawrence that he has been unable to deliver to Romeo the letter which outlines the plan. Lawrence realises the danger and sets off to the Capulet tomb to release Juliet and hide her in his cell until he can make contact with Romeo.

Romeo has already arrived at the vault. Paris, who is mourning there, finds Romeo attempting to smash down the door and believes he is up to no good. Romeo will not be stopped and they fight. Paris is killed and placed inside the tomb. After gazing at Juliet, who still lies drugged, Romeo drinks the poison which acts swiftly. Friar Lawrence cannot save him, but arrives just as Juliet awakes. Afraid of being discovered, he will not stay but Juliet remains. She discovers that Romeo has killed himself by taking the poison and, wishing to die too, she sees if any drops of poison remain. The poison is finished so she stabs herself with Romeo's dagger.

The Watch arrives with the Capulets, the Montagues and the Prince to discover the tragic scene, and it is left to Friar Lawrence to explain the carnage that lies before them. Montague and Capulet are united in their tears and swear to bury their old grudges with their children.

(Opposite) Romeo and Paris: Temba Theatre production, London 1988.

1 *flattering truth of sleep* Romeo knows that you often dream about things you want to happen, rather than reality. Even so he cannot help believing in what he has dreamt.

2 *presage* foretell.

3 *bosom's lord* heart.

lightly happily.

throne the breast.

7 *gives...leave* permits a dead man.

10 *possessed* when you really have it.

18 *monument* tomb.

Act Five

Scene one

A street in Mantua.

Enter ROMEO.

ROMEO
    If I may trust the flattering truth of sleep,
    My dreams presage some joyful news at hand;
    My bosom's lord sits lightly in his throne,
    And all this day an unaccustomed spirit
    Lifts me above the ground with cheerful thoughts.   5
    I dreamt my lady came and found me dead –
    Strange dream, that gives a dead man leave to
       think! –
    And breathed such life with kisses in my lips
    That I revived and was an emperor.
    Ah me! how sweet is love itself possessed,   10
    When but love's shadows are so rich in joy!

Enter BALTHASAR.

    News from Verona! How now, Balthasar?
    Dost thou not bring me letters from the Friar?
    How doth my lady? Is my father well?
    How fares my Juliet? That I ask again,   15
    For nothing can be ill if she be well.

BALTHASAR
    Then she is well, and nothing can be ill.
    Her body sleeps in Capel's monument,
    And her immortal part with angels lives.
    I saw her laid low in her kindred's vault,   20

21 *presently took post*   rode here straightaway.

23 *my office*   my responsibility.

26 *post-horses*   very fast horses could be hired at inns and changed for fresh ones *en route* if it was essential to ride somewhere very quickly.

28 *import*   signify, suggest.

29 *misadventure*   bad luck, disaster.

33 *straight*   shortly.

34 *lie*   as a lover and beside her in the tomb.

35 *Let's see for means*   how am I going to do this?

37 *apothecary*   person who makes up and sells medicines and poisons.

38 *'a*   he.

39 *In tattered...brows*   dressed in ragged clothes and with a gloomy frown.

40 *Culling of simples*   gathering herbs.

Meagre   thin.

42 *needy*   poor.

And presently took post to tell it you.
O pardon me for bringing these ill news,
Since you did leave it for my office, sir.

ROMEO

Is it e'en so? Then I defy you, stars!
Thou knowest my lodging. Get me ink and paper, 25
And hire post-horses. I will hence to-night.

BALTHASAR

I do beseech you, sir, have patience.
Your looks are pale and wild, and do import
Some misadventure.

ROMEO

             Tush, thou art deceived.
Leave me, and do the thing I bid thee do. 30
Hast thou no letters to me from the Friar?

BALTHASAR

No, my good lord.

ROMEO

            No matter; get thee gone,
And hire those horses. I'll be with thee straight.

                    Exit BALTHASAR

Well, Juliet, I will lie with thee to-night.
Let's see for means. O mischief, thou art swift 35
To enter in the thoughts of desperate men!
I do remember an apothecary,
And hereabouts 'a dwells, which late I noted
In tattered weeds, with overwhelming brows,
Culling of simples. Meagre were his looks: 40
Sharp misery had worn him to the bones;
And in his needy shop a tortoise hung,

45 *beggarly account*   poor selection.

46 *bladders*   containers holding liquid.

47 *packthread*   strong twine or thread used for sewing packages.

cakes of roses   block of compressed rose petals used for perfume.

48 *show*   display.

49 *penury*   poverty.

51 *Whose sale is present death*   the sale of which carries immediate sentence of death.

52 *caitiff*   mean, despicable.

53 *forerun my need*   came into my head long before I needed it.

56 *holiday*   holy day, feast day when people took time off work.

59 *ducats*   gold or silver coins.

60 *soon-speeding gear*   swift-acting stuff.

61 *disperse*   spread.

63 *the trunk...of breath*   the body may stop breathing.

64 *hasty powder*   very explosive gunpowder.

66 *mortal*   deadly.

67 *he*   person.

utters   sells.

An alligator stuffed, and other skins
Of ill-shaped fishes; and about his shelves
A beggarly account of empty boxes,   45
Green earthen pots, bladders, and musty seeds,
Remnants of packthread, and old cakes of roses,
Were thinly scattered to make up a show.
Noting this penury, to myself I said:
"An if a man did need a poison now,   50
Whose sale is present death in Mantua,
Here lives a caitiff wretch would sell it him."
O this same thought did but forerun my need,
And this same needy man must sell it me.
As I remember, this should be the house.   55
Being holiday, the beggar's shop is shut.
What ho! apothecary!

Enter APOTHECARY.

APOTHECARY

                    Who calls so loud?

ROMEO

Come hither, man. I see that thou art poor.
(*He shows him a bag of money*) Hold, there is forty
    ducats: let me have
A dram of poison, such soon-speeding gear   60
As will disperse itself through all the veins,
That the life-weary taker may fall dead,
And that the trunk may be discharged of breath
As violently as hasty powder fired
Doth hurry from the fatal cannon's womb.   65

APOTHECARY

Such mortal drugs I have, but Mantua's law
Is death to any he that utters them.

68 *bare*   poor.

70 *starveth in thy eyes*   your hunger shows in your eyes.

71 *Contempt...back*   your clothes are so tattered that you must be despised and thought a beggar.

73 *affords*   has.

74 *break it*   break the law (and break out of your poverty).

79 *dispatch you straight*   kill you instantly.

82 *compounds*   concoctions.

84 *get thyself in flesh*   put some weight on, fatten yourself up.

85 *cordial*   medicine or drink for reviving the spirits.

ROMEO

Art thou so bare and full of wretchedness,
And fear'st to die? Famine is in thy cheeks;
Need and oppression starveth in thy eyes,   70
Contempt and beggary hangs upon thy back.
The world is not thy friend, nor the world's law:
The world affords no law to make the rich;
Then be not poor, but break it and take this.

APOTHECARY

(*Taking the money*) My poverty, but not my will
   consents.   75

ROMEO

I pay thy poverty and not thy will.

APOTHECARY

(*Giving him the poison*) Put this in any liquid thing
   you will
And drink it off, and if you had the strength
Of twenty men, it would dispatch you straight.

ROMEO

There is thy gold: worse poison to men's souls,   80
Doing more murder in this loathsome world,
Than these poor compounds that thou may'st not
   sell.
I sell thee poison: thou hast sold me none.
Farewell; buy food, and get thyself in flesh.

                                    Exit APOTHECARY

Come, cordial and not poison, go with me   85
To Juliet's grave, for there must I use thee.

                                              Exit

4   *if his mind be writ*   if he has sent me a written message of his thoughts.

5   *barefoot brother*   Franciscan friar, who always travelled with bare feet.

6   *order*   religious community.

    associate me   go with me, keep me company.

8   *searchers*   coroners (who examined dead bodies to find out why someone had died).

10   *infectious pestilence*   bubonic plague, a common fatal illness in Elizabethan times.

11   *Sealed up the doors*   confined them to quarantine within the house.

12   *stayed*   prevented.

13   *bare*   bore, delivered.

14   *here it is again*   I still have it here.

17   *brotherhood*   religious order.

18   *nice*   trivial, petty.

18–19   *full of charge...import*   full of very important instructions.

Scene two

Friar Lawrence's cell.

Enter FRIAR JOHN.

FRIAR JOHN
Holy Franciscan! Friar! brother, ho!

Enter FRIAR LAWRENCE *from his inner room.*

FRIAR LAWRENCE
This same should be the voice of Friar John.
Welcome from Mantua. What says Romeo?
Or, if his mind be writ, give me his letter.

FRIAR JOHN
Going to find a barefoot brother out, 5
One of our order, to associate me
Here in this city visiting the sick,
And finding him, the searchers of the town,
Suspecting that we both were in a house
Where the infectious pestilence did reign, 10
Sealed up the doors, and would not let us forth,
So that my speed to Mantua there was stayed.

FRIAR LAWRENCE
Who bare my letter then to Romeo?

FRIAR JOHN
I could not send it – here it is again –
Nor get a messenger to bring it thee, 15
So fearful were they of infection.

FRIAR LAWRENCE
Unhappy fortune! By my brotherhood,
The letter was not nice, but full of charge
Of dear import, and the neglecting it

20 *danger* harm.

21 *crow* crowbar.

24 *must I to* I must go to.

26 *beshrew* scold, curse.

27 *Hath had...accidents* has not received the news of what has happened.

1 *Hence...aloof* go and stand far off.

3 *lay thee all along* lie flat.

5 *So shall...tread* no one shall set foot in the churchyard.

7 *But thou shalt hear it* without your being bound to hear the sound of it.

May do much danger. Friar John, go hence;   20
Get me an iron crow, and bring it straight
Unto my cell.

FRIAR JOHN
Brother, I'll go and bring it thee.

Exit FRIAR JOHN

FRIAR LAWRENCE
Now must I to the monument alone.
Within this three hours will fair Juliet wake.   25
She will beshrew me much that Romeo
Hath had no notice of these accidents.
But I will write again to Mantua,
And keep her at my cell till Romeo come.
Poor living corse, closed in a dead man's tomb!   30

Exit

Scene three

The Capulets' vault.

Enter PARIS *and his* PAGE *at the entrance.*

PARIS
Give me thy torch, boy. Hence, and stand aloof.
Yet put it out for I would not be seen.
Under yond yew trees lay thee all along,
Holding thy ear close to the hollow ground,
So shall no foot upon the churchyard tread,   5
Being loose, unfirm with digging up of graves,
But thou shalt hear it. Whistle then to me,
As signal that thou hear'st something approach.
Give me those flowers. Do as I bid thee, go.

11 *adventure*   risk it.

12 *strew*   cover.

13 canopy   curtain over a bed, or in this case, Paris' poetic word for the cover over the tomb.

14 *sweet...dew*   sprinkle with perfume every night.

15 *wanting that*   if I have no perfume.

distilled by moans   made out of my moans.

16 *obsequies*   funeral observances, rituals.

20 *cross*   interrupt, disturb.

21 *Muffle*   hide.

22 *mattock*   type of spade.

23 *Hold*   wait.

27 *my course*   what I decide to do.

PAGE

> (*Aside*) I am almost afraid to stand alone   10
> Here in the churchyard, yet I will adventure.

He hides behind the trees.

PARIS

> (*To* JULIET) Sweet flower, with flowers thy bridal bed
>   I strew –
> O woe, thy canopy is dust and stones –
> Which with sweet water nightly I will dew,
> Or, wanting that, with tears distilled by moans.   15
> The obsequies that I for thee will keep,
> Nightly shall be to strew thy grave and weep.

The PAGE *whistles.*

> The boy gives warning; something doth approach.
> What cursèd foot wanders this way to-night,
> To cross my obsequies and true love's rite?   20
> What, with a torch? Muffle me, night, a while.

He hides in the churchyard.

Enter ROMEO *and* BALTHASAR *with a torch, mattock and crowbar.*

ROMEO

> Give me that mattock and the wrenching iron.
> Hold, take this letter; early in the morning
> See thou deliver it to my lord and father.
> Give me the light. Upon thy life I charge thee,   25
> Whate'er thou hear'st or seest, stand all aloof,
> And do not interrupt me in my course.
> Why I descend into this bed of death
> Is partly to behold my lady's face,
> But chiefly to take thence from her dead finger   30
> A precious ring, a ring that I must use

32 *In dear employment*   for a special purpose.

33 *jealous*   suspicious.

36 *hungry*   greedy (for bodies of the dead).

37 *intents*   intentions.

38 *inexorable*   relentless.

39 *empty*   hungry.

43 *hereabout*   nearby.

44 *I doubt*   I am suspicious of.

45 *maw*   belly.

46 *dearest morsel*   most delicious food, meaning Juliet.

47 *enforce*   force.

48 *in despite*   in spite of the fact that you are already full.

53 *apprehend*   stop.

In dear employment. Therefore hence, be gone.
But if thou, jealous, dost return to pry
In what I farther shall intend to do,
By heaven, I will tear thee joint by joint,   35
And strew this hungry churchyard with thy limbs.
The time and my intents are savage, wild,
More fierce and more inexorable far
Than empty tigers or the roaring sea.

BALTHASAR

I will be gone, sir, and not trouble ye.   40

ROMEO

So shalt thou show me friendship. (*Gives him money*)
    Take thou that.
Live and be prosperous; and farewell, good fellow.

BALTHASAR

(*Aside*) For all this same, I'll hide me hereabout.
His looks I fear, and his intents I doubt.

He withdraws and hides in the churchyard.

ROMEO

(*He smashes at the gate with the crowbar*) Thou detest-
    able maw, thou womb of death   45
Gorged with the dearest morsel of the earth;
Thus I enforce thy rotten jaws to open,
And in despite I'll cram thee with more food.

PARIS

This is that banished haughty Montague
That murdered my love's cousin, with which grief 50
It is supposed the fair creature died,
And here is come to do some villainous shame
To the dead bodies. I will apprehend him.

54 *unhallowed*   unholy, wicked.

58 *therefore came I hither*   that is why I came here.

59 *tempt not*   don't provoke.

60 *these gone*   the people who are buried there.

61 *affright*   scare you away.

65 *armed against myself*   Romeo is carrying (armed with) the poison with which he intends to kill himself.

68 *defy your conjurations*   ignore your requests.

69 *for a felon*   as a criminal.

71 *watch*   patrol who police the city during the night.

74 *peruse*   look carefully at.

He comes forward.

> Stop thy unhallowed toil, vile Montague!
> Can vengeance be pursued further than death?   55
> Condemnèd villain, I do apprehend thee.
> Obey, and go with me, for thou must die.

ROMEO

> I must indeed, and therefore came I hither.
> Good gentle youth, tempt not a desperate man.
> Fly hence and leave me. Think upon these gone;   60
> Let them affright thee. I beseech thee, youth,
> Put not another sin upon my head
> By urging me to fury. O be gone!
> By heaven, I love thee better than myself
> For I come hither armed against myself.   65
> Stay not, be gone; live, and hereafter say
> A madman's mercy bid thee run away.

PARIS

> I do defy thy conjurations
> And apprehend thee for a felon here.

ROMEO

> Wilt thou provoke me? Then have at thee, boy!   70

They fight.

PAGE

> O Lord, they fight! I will go call the watch.

> *Exit* PAGE

PARIS

> (*Falling*) O I am slain! If thou be merciful,
> Open the tomb; lay me with Juliet.

ROMEO

> In faith, I will. Let me peruse this face,

76 *betossèd soul*   preoccupied mind.

77 *attend him*   listen to him.

82 *One writ...book*   you, whose name is written down with mine in the book that tells of sad misfortune's victims.

84 *a lantern*   not a dark gloomy place, but one lit up by the brightness of Juliet's beauty.

86 *feasting presence*   chamber in which royalty would receive guests, here described as festive and decorated.

87 *by a dead man interred*   buried by a man who will soon be dead too.

89 *keepers*   gaolers or nurses.

90 *lightning*   sudden change of mood to light-heartedness.

94 *ensign*   flag, standard.

96 *not advancèd there*   has not reached it yet.

97 *bloody sheet*   blood-stained shroud.

99 *in twain*   in two.

100 *To sunder his that*   to split apart the youthfulness of the man who.

103 *unsubstantial*   without shape or substance.

104 *abhorrèd*   hated, repugnant.

105 *paramour*   mistress.

Mercutio's kinsman, noble County Paris! 75
What said my man when my betossèd soul
Did not attend him as we rode? I think
He told me Paris should have married Juliet.
Said he not so? Or did I dream it so?
Or am I mad, hearing him talk of Juliet, 80
To think it was so? O give me thy hand,
One writ with me in sour misfortune's book.
I'll bury thee in a triumphant grave.
A grave? O no, a lantern, slaughtered youth;
For here lies Juliet, and her beauty makes 85
This vault a feasting presence full of light.
Death, lie thou there, by a dead man interred.

He lays PARIS *beside* JULIET's *tomb.*

How oft when men are at the point of death
Have they been merry, which their keepers call
A lightning before death! O, how may I 90
Call this a lightning? O my love, my wife!
Death, that hath sucked the honey of thy breath,
Hath had no power yet upon thy beauty.
Thou art not conquered; beauty's ensign yet
Is crimson in thy lips and in thy cheeks, 95
And death's pale flag is not advancèd there.
Tybalt, liest thou there in thy bloody sheet?
O, what more favour can I do to thee
Than with that hand that cut thy youth in twain
To sunder his that was thine enemy? 100
Forgive me, cousin. Ah, dear Juliet,
Why art thou yet so fair? Shall I believe
That unsubstantial Death is amorous,
And that the lean abhorrèd monster keeps
Thee here in dark to be his paramour? 105
For fear of that I still will stay with thee,

107 *pallet*   hard bed.

111 *shake the yoke...stars*   shake off the weight of my unlucky life.

115 *A dateless...Death*   an everlasting bargain with all-consuming Death.

116 *conduct*   someone who guides or escorts.

  unsavoury   foul-tasting (Romeo is speaking to the poison).

117 *pilot*   navigator.

  run on   run aground on, shipwrecked on.

118 *bark*   ship.

119 *true*   faithful to your word.

125 *yond*   over there.

126 *discern*   can make out, see.

And never from this pallet of dim night
Depart again. Here, here will I remain,
With worms that are thy chambermaids. O, here
Will I set up my everlasting rest,   110
And shake the yoke of inauspicious stars
From this world-wearied flesh. Eyes, look your last;
Arms take your last embrace; and lips, O you,
The doors of breath, seal with a righteous kiss
A dateless bargain to engrossing Death.   115
Come, bitter conduct; come, unsavoury guide,
Thou desperate pilot, now at once run on
The dashing rocks thy seasick weary bark.
Here's to my love. (*Drinks the poison*) O true
    apothecary!
Thy drugs are quick. Thus with a kiss I die.   120

He dies

Enter FRIAR LAWRENCE *at the gate of the vault, with a lantern, crowbar and spade.*

FRIAR LAWRENCE
Saint Francis be my speed! How oft to-night
Have my old feet stumbled at graves! Who's there?

BALTHASAR
Here's one, a friend, and one that knows you well.

FRIAR LAWRENCE
Bliss be upon you. Tell me, good my friend,
What torch is yond that vainly lends his light   125
To grubs and eyeless skulls? As I discern
It burneth in the Capels' monument.

BALTHASAR
It doth so, holy sir; and there's my master,
One that you love.

132 *knows not but*   thinks that.

133 *menace*   threaten.

136 *ill unthrifty thing*   awful ill-fated event.

142 *masterless and gory*   bloody and without their owners.

143 *discoloured*   stained.

FRIAR LAWRENCE

Who is it?

BALTHASAR

Romeo.

FRIAR LAWRENCE

How long hath he been there?

BALTHASAR

Full half an hour.   130

FRIAR LAWRENCE

Go with me to the vault.

BALTHASAR

I dare not, sir.
My master knows not but I am gone hence,
And fearfully did menace me with death
If I did stay to look on his intents.

FRIAR LAWRENCE

Stay then; I'll go alone. Fear comes upon me.   135
O much I fear some ill unthrifty thing.

BALTHASAR

As I did sleep under this yew tree here,
I dreamt my master and another fought,
And that my master slew him.

FRIAR LAWRENCE

Romeo!
Alack, alack, what blood is this which stains   140
The stony entrance of this sepulchre?
What mean these masterless and gory swords
To lie discoloured by this place of peace?

He enters the vault.

145 *steeped in* soaked with.

    unkind cruel.

146 *guilty of this lamentable chance!* can be blamed for this tragic occurrence.

148 *comfortable* reassuring.

152 *contagion* contagious illness.

153 *contradict* stand up against.

154 *thwarted our intents* prevented us from doing what we intended.

155 *in thy bosom* by your side.

156 *dispose of* put.

162 *timeless* for evermore, and probably in the sense of badly timed too.

163 *churl* thoughtless creature.

166 *restorative* cure (because it will cure her unhappiness by reuniting – restoring – her with Romeo).

Romeo! O pale! Who else? What, Paris, too?
And steeped in blood? Ah, what an unkind hour   145
Is guilty of this lamentable chance!

JULIET *wakes*.

The lady stirs.

JULIET
O comfortable Friar, where is my lord?
I do remember well where I should be,
And there I am. Where is my Romeo?   150

Approaching voices are heard.

FRIAR LAWRENCE
I hear some noise, lady. Come from that nest
Of death, contagion, and unnatural sleep.
A greater power than we can contradict
Hath thwarted our intents. Come, come away.
Thy husband in thy bosom there lies dead,   155
And Paris too. Come, I'll dispose of thee
Among a sisterhood of holy nuns.
Stay not to question, for the watch is coming.
Come, go, good Juliet; I dare no longer stay.

JULIET
Go, get thee hence, for I will not away.   160

Exit FRIAR LAWRENCE

What's here? A cup closed in my true love's hand?
Poison, I see, hath been his timeless end.
O churl! drunk all, and left no friendly drop
To help me after? I will kiss thy lips:
Haply some poison yet doth hang on them   165
To make me die with a restorative.
(*Kisses him*) Thy lips are warm.

169 *brief* quick.

170 *This is thy sheath* your new sheath is in my breast.

173 *attach* bring them with you, hold them.

179 *woes* sad sights.

180–1 *the true ground...descry* we need further information if we are to understand the dreadful things that have happened here.

The PAGE *and the* WATCH *approach the vault.*

FIRST WATCHMAN
  Lead, boy. Which way?

JULIET
  Yea, noise? Then I'll be brief. (*She takes* ROMEO'S
    dagger) O happy dagger!
  This is thy sheath; there rust, and let me die.   170

            She stabs herself, falls on ROMEO'S *body and dies*

The PAGE *and the* WATCH *enter the vault.*

PAGE
  This is the place; there, where the torch doth burn.

FIRST WATCHMAN
  The ground is bloody. Search about the church-
    yard.
  Go, some of you: whoe'er you find, attach.

                    Some WATCHMEN *go out*

  Pitiful sight! Here lies the County slain,
  And Juliet bleeding, warm and newly dead,   175
  Who here hath lain this two days burièd.
  Go, tell the Prince, run to the Capulets,
  Raise up the Montagues. Some others search.

                    More WATCHMEN *go out*

  We see the ground whereon these woes do lie,
  But the true ground of all these piteous woes   180
  We cannot without circumstance descry.

Re-enter some of the WATCH *with* BALTHASAR.

187 *A great suspicion* very suspicious.

    Stay hold.

188 *misadventure* unfortunate event.

189 *our person* the Prince is speaking of himself.

190 *so shrieked abroad* shouted about in the streets.

194 *What fear...ears* what is the cause of all the commotion which you can hear?

SECOND WATCHMAN
Here's Romeo's man; we found him in the churchyard.

FIRST WATCHMAN
Hold him in safety till the Prince come hither.

Re-enter another WATCHMAN *with* FRIAR LAWRENCE.

THIRD WATCHMAN
Here is a Friar that trembles, sighs, and weeps.
We took this mattock and this spade from him,   185
As he was coming from this churchyard's side.

FIRST WATCHMAN
A great suspicion! Stay the Friar too.

Enter PRINCE ESCALUS *and* ATTENDANTS.

PRINCE
What misadventure is so early up,
That calls our person from our morning rest?

Enter CAPULET *and* LADY CAPULET.

CAPULET
What should it be that is so shrieked abroad?   190

LADY CAPULET
O, the people in the streets cry "Romeo",
Some "Juliet", and some "Paris", and all run
With open outcry toward our monument.

PRINCE
What fear is this which startles in your ears?

FIRST WATCHMAN
Sovereign, here lies the County Paris slain;   195
And Romeo dead; and Juliet, dead before,
Warm and new killed.

198 *comes*   has occurred.

200 *instruments*   tools.

203 *mista'en*   been put in the wrong place.

his house   its sheath.

207 *warns my old age to a sepulchre*   makes me feel old, summoning me to my grave.

209 *more early down*   gone to sleep even earlier.

210 *is dead tonight*   has died during the night.

212 *What further...age?*   what other sadness has happened to beat down an old man like me?

214 *untaught*   ill-mannered, unschooled in manners.

215 *to press before*   to push past (Montague is saying that children should not die before their parents).

216 *Seal up...a while*   control your grief and anger for the moment.

PRINCE

    Search, seek, and know how this foul murder comes.

FIRST WATCHMAN

    Here is a Friar, and slaughtered Romeo's man,
    With instruments upon them fit to open   200
    These dead men's tombs.

CAPULET

    O heavens! O wife, look how our daughter bleeds!
    This dagger has mista'en, for lo, his house
    Is empty on the back of Montague,
    And is mis-sheathèd in my daughter's bosom.   205

LADY CAPULET

    O me! this sight of death is as a bell
    That warns my old age to a sepulchre.

Enter MONTAGUE.

PRINCE

    Come, Montague; for thou art early up
    To see thy son and heir more early down.

MONTAGUE

    Alas, my liege, my wife is dead to-night;   210
    Grief of my son's exile hath stopped her breath.
    What further woe conspires against mine age?

PRINCE

    Look, and thou shalt see.

MONTAGUE

    (*Seeing* ROMEO) O thou untaught! what manners is
       in this,
    To press before thy father to a grave?   215

PRINCE

    Seal up the mouth of outrage for a while,

217 *clear these ambiguities*   sort out these mysteries.

218 *their spring...descent*   their cause, their origin and how they came to pass.

219 *general of your woes*   lead you in mourning.

220 *forbear*   hold back.

221 *let mischance...patience*   be patient in spite of the dreadful misfortunes that have occurred.

222 *parties of suspicion*   those people who are suspects.

223 *greatest*   most likely suspect.

225 *make against me*   suggest that I am guilty.

226 *to impeach and purge*   accuse and excuse.

228 *in*   about, concerning.

229 *short date of breath*   the life I have left to live.

233 *stolen*   secret.

234 *doomsday*   the day of reckoning, the day of his death.

238 *Betrothed*   promised her in marriage.

perforce   by force (against her wishes).

240 *devise some mean*   think up some way.

243 *tutored by my art*   guided by my skill (in herbalism and medicine).

Till we can clear these ambiguities,
And know their spring, their head, their true
   descent,
And then will I be general of your woes,
And lead you even to death. Meantime forbear,   220
And let mischance be slave to patience.
Bring forth the parties of suspicion.

FRIAR LAWRENCE *and* BALTHASAR *are brought forward.*

FRIAR LAWRENCE
I am the greatest; able to do least,
Yet most suspected, as the time and place
Doth make against me, of this direful murder;   225
And here I stand, both to impeach and purge,
Myself condemnèd and myself excused.

PRINCE
Then say at once what thou dost know in this.

FRIAR LAWRENCE
I will be brief, for my short date of breath
Is not so long as is a tedious tale.   230
Romeo there dead, was husband to that Juliet;
And she, there dead, that Romeo's faithful wife.
I married them; and their stolen marriage day
Was Tybalt's doomsday, whose untimely death
Banished the new-made bridegroom from this city; 235
For whom, and not for Tybalt, Juliet pined.
You, to remove that siege of grief from her,
Betrothed and would have married her perforce
To County Paris. Then comes she to me,
And with wild looks bid me devise some mean   240
To rid her from this second marriage,
Or in my cell there would she kill herself.
Then gave I her, so tutored by my art,

245–6 *wrought on her...death*   made her look as if she was dead.

247 *as*   on.

dire   dreadful.

248 *borrowed*   temporary.

249 *the potion's force should cease*   the effect of the potion should wear off.

251 *stayed*   held up.

253 *prefixèd*   arranged beforehand.

255 *closely*   in secret.

257 *ere*   before.

266 *is privy*   knows all about this.

aught   anything.

267 *Miscarried*   went wrong.

268 *some hour before his time*   before the end of my natural life.

269 *Unto the rigour of severest law*   according to the strictest laws.

270 *still*   always.

273 *in post*   as fast as he could.

A sleeping potion, which so took effect
As I intended, for it wrought on her   245
The form of death. Meantime I writ to Romeo
That he should hither come as this dire night
To help to take her from her borrowed grave,
Being the time the potion's force should cease.
But he which bore my letter, Friar John,   250
Was stayed by accident, and yesternight
Returned my letter back. Then all alone,
At the prefixèd hour of her waking,
Came I to take her from her kindred's vault,
Meaning to keep her closely at my cell   255
Till I conveniently could send to Romeo.
But when I came, some minute ere the time
Of her awakening, here untimely lay
The noble Paris and true Romeo dead.
She wakes, and I entreated her come forth   260
And bear this work of heaven with patience;
But then a noise did scare me from the tomb,
And she, too desperate, would not go with me,
But, as it seems, did violence on herself.
All this I know, and to the marriage   265
Her Nurse is privy, and if aught in this
Miscarried by my fault, let my old life
Be sacrified some hour before his time
Unto the rigour of severest law.

PRINCE

We still have known thee for a holy man.   270
Where's Romeo's man? What can he say to this?

BALTHASAR

I brought my master news of Juliet's death,
And then in post he came from Mantua
To this same place, to this same monument.

275 *early*   as soon as I could.

277 *If I departed not*   unless I went away.

280 *what made your master*   what was your master up to?

283 *Anon*   soon.

ope   open.

284 *drew on him*   drew his sword on him.

286 *make good*   back up, verify.

289 *therewithal*   with the poison.

292 *scourge*   punishment.

294 *winking at your discords*   ignoring your quarrels.

295 *a brace*   a pair.

297 *jointure*   marriage settlement, dowry.

This letter he early bid me give his father,   275
And threatened me with death, going in the vault,
If I departed not and left him there.

PRINCE

Give me the letter; I will look on it.
Where is the County's page that raised the watch?

PAGE *comes forward.*

Sirrah, what made your master in this place?   280

PAGE

He came with flowers to strew his lady's grave,
And bid me stand aloof, and so I did.
Anon comes one with light to ope the tomb,
And by and by my master drew on him,
And then I ran away to call the watch.   285

PRINCE

This letter doth make good the Friar's words,
Their course of love, the tidings of her death;
And here he writes that he did buy a poison
Of a poor 'pothecary, and therewithal
Came to this vault, to die and lie with Juliet.   290
Where be these enemies, Capulet, Montague?
See what a scourge is laid upon your hate,
That heaven finds means to kill your joys with
     love.
And I, for winking at your discords too,
Have lost a brace of kinsmen. All are punished.   295

CAPULET

O brother Montague, give me thy hand.
This is my daughter's jointure, for no more
Can I demand.

300 *whiles* whilst.
301 *at such rate be set* so highly valued.
304 *Poor* unfortunate.
305 *glooming* sad.

MONTAGUE

But I can give thee more,
For I will raise her statue in pure gold,
That whiles Verona by that name is known,   300
There shall no figure at such rate be set
As that of true and faithful Juliet.

CAPULET

As rich shall Romeo's by his lady's lie –
Poor sacrifices of our enmity.

PRINCE

A glooming peace this morning with it brings;   305
The sun for sorrow will not show his head.
Go hence, to have more talk of these sad things.
Some shall be pardoned, and some punishèd;
For never was a story of more woe
Than this of Juliet and her Romeo.   310

Exeunt

Study programme for Key Stage 4

Before reading the play

An old story

The story of the two 'star-crossed' lovers in Shakespeare's *Romeo and Juliet* was not entirely his own brainchild. It comes from a much older story which Shakespeare adapted for the plot of his play. Its original source may have been Greek (although this is not certain) and versions exist in Italian and French. The playwright, however, was probably most familiar with the poem called *The Tragical Historye of Romeus and Juliet* which was written by Arthur Brooke and published in 1562. The difference between Shakespeare's re-telling of the story and that of Brooke lies chiefly in the characters and their motives, for the events are very similar. Brooke wrote a poem which warned young people to beware of lustful desire, whilst Shakespeare examined the complexity of love in its many forms. Where Brooke showed his disapproval of those who disobey their parents, Shakespeare seemed to say disobedience was justified if it was in the name of love and honesty.

Changing old stories to suit a new purpose is one of Shakespeare's techniques and he uses it in many of his plays. His skill as a playwright lies in his ability to handle these well-known stories in ways which capture the emotions and the sympathies of his audience.

Romeo and Juliet sounds like a simple story: boy meets girl, family quarrels and circumstances beyond their control prevent their revealing their love, unfortunate accidents and misunderstandings when they try to be together lead to their deaths by suicide. Yet there is much more to the story than this, and some of the situations in which the lovers find themselves could be – if you were unlucky – ones in which you might find yourself.

▣ Before you begin to read the play, think yourself into the following situations, trying to imagine and express what your emotions might be (you could write a short story or present a role play):

- You fall hopelessly in love with someone you've just met – and then discover that your parents and his or hers are arch-enemies.
- You have to marry someone of your parents' choice, even though you don't want to.

These are the problems the young lovers have to face, but could it have happened anywhere and at any time? Some directors have envisaged the lovers still in medieval Italy and others have attempted to bring them into the twentieth century – a most famous adaptation of the story was Leonard Bernstein's 1950's *West Side Story*, set in America. Romeo and Juliet refuse to remain in the past because their story has a timelessness and raises issues which are still relevant today.

An ardent lover

It is useful to note that the characters in the play vary from stereotypical clowns to psychologically accurate individuals. In Shakespeare's day, both in the theatre and in literature, audiences and readers expected to be introduced to certain types of character. These characters were expected to behave in particular conventional ways, and often to have specific, recognisable physical characteristics. Perhaps the simplest way to imagine this is in the traditional Punch and Judy show (itself derived from the staged productions of the *Commedia dell'arte*) or the typically British pantomime. Audiences would feel cheated without the appearance of the wicked uncle or stepmother, a furious Mr Punch or a bumbling policeman. Soap operas on television also have their share of stereotypes.

It is probably true to say that even today we expect people who are in love to behave in a particular way. We will expect to see them daydreaming or acting absent-mindedly. They will probably not want to eat or sleep very much. They will be constantly thinking or even talking about the one they love.

The character of the lover in Elizabethan drama was even more well-defined and fixed than this. He (for it usually was a man) drew his characteristic appearance and behaviour from the lovers in courtly romances. Shakespeare summed up the absurdity of the lover's character briefly in another of his plays – *As You Like It:*

> And then the lover,
> Sighing like furnace, with a woful ballad
> Made to his mistress' eyebrow,

(Act 2, scene 7, lines 147–9)

When we hear of Romeo he behaves in exactly this manner:

> Many a morning hath he there been seen,
> With tears augmenting the fresh morning's dew,
> Adding to clouds more clouds with his deep sighs;

(Act 1, scene 1, lines 129–31)

His friends tease him because of it, for they realise he is doing little more than acting out the part of the lover. However, never one to follow tradition rigidly, Shakespeare handles Romeo's character carefully, developing his hero to the point where we can no longer make fun of him and are convinced of his real passion for Juliet. At the height of Romeo's expression of his true love a second lover, Paris, takes on the role of stereotype, acting as Romeo once did, and the contrast is complete. Paris cannot break the mould of conventional lover and we are therefore never convinced either of his love for Juliet or his grief at her death.

2   Before meeting the other characters in *Romeo and Juliet* think about the ways in which we expect characters in books, plays and on television to behave. Concentrate on the stereotypical features of the people listed below. Your ideas and discussions could lead to written character descriptions, or acted scenes or monologues:

- the parents of a teenager;
- a religious or spiritual leader;
- a close friend;
- a servant.

A dutiful daughter

Juliet's dilemma is not one which is easy for all of us to understand today. Naturally, few of us escape from disagreements with our parents over one thing or another, but only a handful of us will be asked to make the decision she has to in Act 1, scene 3.

LADY CAPULET
>   Tell me, daughter Juliet,
> How stands your dispositions to be married?

JULIET
> It is an honour that I dream not of.

(lines 62–4)

LADY CAPULET
> Well, think of marriage now. Younger than you,
> Here in Verona, ladies of esteem,
> Are made already mothers.

(lines 67–9)

Those of us who live within a cultural atmosphere where arranged marriages are the norm will find it easier to see that Juliet's parents are not making unreasonable demands upon her at all. In Shakespeare's England only the very rich would marry for the purposes of political or financial alliance.

Many societies have now largely abandoned the practice of arranging marriages for their children and in many instances it is usual to marry the person of your own choice.

Regardless of our cultural heritage, however, we can still easily recognise the problem that thirteen-year-old Juliet faces in Act 3, scene 5 in refusing to bow to her parents wishes after all:

JULIET
> I wonder at this haste, that I must wed
> Ere he that should be my husband comes to woo.
> I pray you tell my lord and father, madam,
> I will not marry yet;

(lines 117–20)

LORD CAPULET
> ... fettle your fine joints 'gainst Thursday next,
> To go with Paris to Saint Peter's Church,
> Or I will drag thee on a hurdle thither.

(lines 152–4)

Juliet's problem is not one of disobeying her parents through her own wilfulness. Because of the families' quarrels she cannot reveal the truth so she has no choice. She must refuse to marry or break the law of the land and the Christian Church by committing an act of bigamy. Her only way out of the situation is to deceive her parents and she does not do this lightly. We can all appreciate her difficult predicament by thinking of times when we have wanted to deceive our parents to get out of a tricky situation. Juliet is not a rebel, but a dutiful daughter who has acted hastily. She is also very young.

☐ It is essential that before we judge either Juliet's actions or her parents, we should take time to consider the positions of all those involved. Spend some time discussing the advantages and disadvantages of:

- arranged marriages;
- marrying for love alone;
- marrying at a very early age;
- marrying too soon after meeting someone.

An ancient grudge

To understand the play fully it is important to appreciate that the romance is set against a backdrop of conflict in the city of Verona in Italy. The Prologue, which introduces the action, tells us that the Capulet and Montague families have for many years been at odds with one another. The origin of the feud is never made clear but this has no relevance to events in the play. It is enough for us to know that they quarrel, and quarrel violently.

In Elizabethan drama, Italians were frequently portrayed as hot-tempered, 'swaggering swordsmen', itching to duel with whoever crossed them. Whilst expecting to see stereotypical Italians, the Elizabethan play-goer would also have been able to identify with the idea of honour – if you were insulted in the street, it was an insult to your honour and you defended it in any way you knew how. (Christopher Marlowe, a playwright and contemporary of Shakespeare, died from his wounds following just such a quarrel.)

Loyalty also ran high: a servant or an employee was just as likely to become involved in the feud as a member of the family. 'An eye for an eye, a tooth for a tooth' seems to have been the maxim followed by all at this time.

The tragedy of *Romeo and Juliet* takes place as a consequence of this conflict. Juliet's parents wish to provide her with a husband from a rich and influential family. Romeo fits this description exactly if we are to believe that the households are 'both alike in dignity', yet the relationship between the two families does not allow for this possibility. The lovers are unable to reveal their love for one another because of the 'ancient grudge'. Juliet realises this almost immediately, for she says:

> My only love sprung from my only hate!
> Too early seen unknown, and known too late!
> Prodigious birth of love it is to me,
> That I must love a loathèd enemy.

(Act 1, scene 5, lines 138–41)

Neither Romeo, nor Juliet, nor their accomplices – the Nurse and Friar Lawrence – can envisage an end to the hostilities. Circumstances are beyond their control and they take what seems to them the only course of action available, tragic though it turns out to be. The irony is that only the deaths of these two young lovers can finally 'bury their parents' strife'.

During reading

Act 1

Check your knowledge of Act 1

- What do we learn about Benvolio in this act?
- Why do you think Shakespeare changes from prose to blank verse at line 62 in scene 1?
- What are your first impressions of Tybalt?
- How do you think the players on the stage should react when the Prince speaks to them?
- How would you describe Romeo's mood when he first appears on stage? In what way have we been prepared for this?

- What is Capulet's attitude towards his daughter, Juliet? Try to describe what you think their relationship is like, based on the things Capulet says about her. How does he feel about the idea of her marriage?

- What impression do you get of the Nurse?

- How does Juliet react to the suggestion that she should think about being married soon?

- How does Mercutio's character contrast with those of Benvolio and Romeo?

- Why does Juliet ask her Nurse the names of other men before that of Romeo?

Questioning the text in Act 1

1. Study the Prologue carefully and note what it tells you. How would you tell this to someone in your own words? Write your own modern version either in prose or – if you are feeling more ambitious – in poetry. When writing poetry remember that you can use rhyme, blank verse or free verse.

2. What do you make of Sampson and Gregory? Write 'thumbnail' character sketches of them. If this is your second reading, try to explain their significance to the play as a whole.

3. The Prince's speech could be delivered in a number of ways. With a group of friends attempt several different ways of speaking it aloud: you could begin with a blustering prince, try a panicky version, speak it quietly but with authority, deliver it as an old man, act vigorously etc.

   How does the delivery alter the effect of the lines? Would it affect the behaviour of the others on stage? Can you agree on the best way to play this character?

4. Read through Romeo's speech in scene 1, lines 169–81 and then attempt to make up some of your own oxymorons (see 'Shakespeare's language', page xxi). Try to write them into a story or poem.

5 Shakespeare makes much use of recurring imagery in the play: darkness and light, the stars, boats and navigation. Think about the ideas you associate with them. Why do you think they are important to the play? Can you find any others?

As you are reading the play, look out for quotations which contain a recurring theme. For *darkness* and *light*, for example, you might jot down: '... look to behold this night Earth-treading stars that make dark heaven light'.

Draw up a table of these as you meet them, including their act, scene and line references as you may need to refer back to them. Leave a column for any notes you want to make.

image/theme	quotation	reference in play	notes

6 Begin a character map of any major character, recording what is said about them by others. Add to this each time the character is discussed. Include act, scene and line references so that you can refer back later.

7 In Act 1, scene 5, Romeo and Juliet fall in love at first sight. Read through this section of the text again and in small groups discuss how this unlikely event might be made to look convincing on the stage.

Write out director's instructions for setting, movement and lighting. Consider which of these will be most important for your vision of what is happening. Would Shakespeare's company have been able to achieve the same effects?

Act 2

Check your knowledge of Act 2

- In what ways does the chorus which opens this act differ from the first one before Act 1? How is it similar? Would anything be lost if this were not included?

- How would you describe the friendship between Mercutio and Romeo?
- Who is more sympathetic towards Romeo's feelings: Mercutio or Benvolio? What proof do you have of this?
- What is Mercutio's attitude towards women?
- What is Juliet's initial reaction when she realises she has been overheard talking about Romeo?
- What is Juliet worried about in scene 2, line 118?
- What do you think is going through Juliet's mind in scene 2, line 126?
- What mistake does the Friar make when he realises Romeo has not been home all night? Why are we reminded of Romeo's love for Rosaline at this point?
- What reason does the Friar use for assisting Romeo in his venture?
- Can you explain why the Nurse appears not to listen to Romeo properly in scene 4, lines 166–76.
- How does the Friar's last speech differ from his earlier advice to Romeo? Can you suggest any reason for the change?

Questioning the text in Act 2

1. Discuss Mercutio's attitude towards women in scene 1. Do you think that anyone might find his attitude offensive today? Debate the case for either cutting Mercutio's lines, or for leaving them as they are.

2. Working in groups, read through or act out scene 2 from line 48 to the end. Discuss which of the two new lovers is the more practical and which the more romantic at this stage in the play. Refer closely to the text when you give reasons for your answers.

3. Juliet's speech in scene 2, lines 85–106 talks of worries that might also trouble girls today. Write a modern speech for Juliet which develops the same ideas.

4.
> Love goes toward love as schoolboys from their books,
> But love from love, toward school with heavy looks.

(scene 2, lines 156–7)

Construct some of your own similes like those at the bottom of page 319, comparing the parting of lovers with other things.

Act 3

Check your knowledge of Act 3

- Do the lines Mercutio speaks in scene 1, lines 5–34 seem appropriate to describe Benvolio? Of whom might they form a better description?

- Who begins the quarrel which takes place in scene 1?

- Who is to blame for Mercutio's death?

- What does Lady Capulet want the Prince to do about Tybalt's death?

- There are presumably a number of witnesses to the fight. Why, then, does the Prince ask Benvolio to explain what has happened?

- After all she has said about Romeo in scene 2, why does the Nurse offer to go to find him for Juliet?

- What do the Friar's words in scene 3, line 83 suggest about a) Romeo's behaviour and b) the Friar's opinion of it?

- How would you describe the difference between Juliet's reaction to Tybalt's death and that of her father? How could you explain this difference?

- Capulet seems very certain that Juliet will do as he wishes (in scene 4, line 14). What do we know that will prove him wrong?

- Why are Juliet's words in scene 5, lines 84–5 ironic?

Questioning the text in Act 3

1 What difficulties might a director have with the two fight sequences in scene 1? Discuss these and then work out effective movements for both of them, thinking particularly about the length of time you would want them to last. What difficulties did you encounter?

2 Describe as accurately as you can the change in mood between the end of scene 1 and the beginning of scene 2. Prepare detailed instructions for set and lighting designers on how you would wish this change to be represented on stage.

3 Shakespeare has very carefully patterned the sequence of scenes in this play. Which other scene does scene 2 remind you of? Working in pairs draw up a list to show how the scenes are similar and how they differ. Discuss the effect of this and other scene patterns you come across.

4 Write a soliloquy (in modern English) for Juliet to speak after the Nurse leaves her at the end of scene 2. Pay particular attention to what she might be thinking and feeling towards her parents at this point.

5 Ah Sir! Ah sir! Death's the end of all. (scene 3, line 91)

With a partner, experiment with ways in which this line could be spoken by the Nurse. How do you think it is meant to sound and what do you think she is really trying to say?

6 In scene 4 Paris tells us that today is Monday. Checking back carefully for references to times of the day and night make a time line, including all the major events, from the start of the play until now. Continue it as you read. It will be useful to you when doing the assignments in the 'After reading' section which starts on page 325.

7 Juliet's speech in scene 5, lines 92–101 is very ambiguous. Whilst her mother understands her to be saying one thing, we understand her to be saying another.

With a partner work out how you could get these double meanings across, paying particular attention to how you will deal with the punctuation.

8 Discuss what Juliet means by 'Amen' in scene 5, line 228 and how this differs from what the Nurse believes she means.

Act 4

Check your knowledge of Act 4

- What is the Friar attempting to do in his conversation with Paris at the start of scene 1?

- What do we learn about Paris through his manners and behaviour in this act?
- Capulet does not explain why he wants to bring the wedding forward by a whole day. What reason can you suggest?
- How will the change in the wedding arrangements affect the Friar's plans for Juliet?
- In scene 2 Capulet believes that Juliet has obeyed him and that their earlier quarrel has been made up. What is the truth of the matter?
- Scene 3 is one of the many in which we see the Nurse with Juliet. What is different about this scene? How would you describe the relationship of Juliet and the Nurse a) in the past and b) now?
- After the discovery of Juliet's apparent death in scene 5, Lady Capulet, the Nurse, Paris and Capulet all make speeches of mourning. Look at these closely. What does each speech tell us about the character who utters it and their relationship to Juliet?
- Why is the Friar in such a hurry to get Juliet buried?
- We do not see the Nurse again after this act. Given that she has played such a prominent part up until now, why do you think she disappears from the action? Of which other character have we already lost sight?

Questioning the text in Act 4

1. Scene 1 shows the only meeting between Juliet and Paris in the play. Working in pairs, discuss what you know about them and mime the meeting, aiming to show their facial expressions and gestures as clearly as possible. When you think you have it right, add in their words, this time attempting to get the tone of voice right.

2. In scene 5 it is the Nurse who discovers Juliet's apparently lifeless body. It could, however, have been her mother or father. Write the script for an alternative scene in which either one or both of them discovers her first. Think carefully about how their reactions might be different in this case.

3. As was the custom, Paris was to arrive at the Capulet's house on the wedding morning accompanied by music to serenade Juliet.

Research and tape some music which would be appropriate for the occasion. Explain your choice to the rest of the class.

4 Scene 5 could be considered to be very melodramatic and a modern audience might find a shorter scene more convincing.

In small groups discuss which of the lines of mourning you would cut and which you consider to be the most important things said once Juliet's body is discovered.

5 As in many of his plays, at the end of Act 4 Shakespeare surprisingly introduces playful humour at a time of great sorrow. This may seem to be inappropriate from a modern viewpoint but was quite acceptable to the Elizabethan audience. Decide what the musicians and Peter add to the last scene and whether you would include this or omit it if you were to stage the play. Consider also what it reveals about Shakespeare as a playwright.

Act 5

Check your knowledge of Act 5

- What mood is Romeo in when he enters? How do you react to Romeo's first speech in this act?

- Why is the apothecary reluctant to sell poison to Romeo in scene 1?

- Apart from offering the apothecary money, what means does Romeo use to persuade the man to sell the poison to him?

- How important is it that in scene 2 Friar John gives the full explanation for why the letter was not delivered to Romeo? How much of this do we really need to know? How much of it do we know already?

- In scene 3, why does Romeo tell Balthasar that he is going into Juliet's tomb merely to retrieve a ring he gave her? If it were the truth, why would he want to take the ring from her finger at this stage? Do you think Balthasar believes him?

- Why does Balthasar decide to disobey Romeo and stay near the tomb?

- When Paris sees Romeo in the vault in scene 3, what does he think Romeo is doing? Is he justified in his mistake?
- What does Friar Lawrence plan to do with Juliet when she wakes and Romeo is dead?
- Why does the Friar not stay with Juliet?
- Why is the fact that Juliet's body is still warm odd to those who find her (scene 3, line 175)?
- What new things do we learn about Prince Escalus' character and function in the last scene of the play?
- Does the play have a completely unhappy ending, or is there some joy in it after all?

Questioning the text in Act 5

1 In scene 2 Friar John relates the tale of the delayed letter. Either improvise or write a script for this missing scene. Where would you put it in to the action?

2 As Paris strews flowers on Juliet's grave (scene 3, lines 12–17), he recites the sestet (last six lines) of a sonnet which would have fourteen lines in total. Try to suggest what the first eight lines (octet) of the sonnet might have contained, or with a partner, try to write them.

3 By Act 5, scene 3 Romeo's appearance has probably changed a great deal since we first saw him. Draw before and after sketches of him, basing your drawings on what is said about him at various points in the play.

4 In scene 3, line 130, Balthasar tells us that Romeo has been at the tomb for half an hour. Clearly the action has not taken that long on stage. Suggest ways in which a production might give the impression that this time has passed. Does Balthasar say anything else which could help with your suggestions?

5 The audience does not really need to hear all of Friar Lawrence's speech in scene 3 lines 229–69. Many modern productions reduce it quite substantially. Decide whether you would do this and if so which lines it would be essential to keep and why.

After reading

Plot

In Assignment 6 of 'Questioning the text in Act 3' on page 321, you are asked to make a time line including all the major events in the play. Use this to help you complete the following activities.

▣ Brooke's *Romeus and Juliet* was the source of the basic tale behind Shakespeare's play. The time scale, however, differs greatly in Brooke's version: the action takes about nine months; Tybalt and Paris are introduced much later in the story and after the ball Romeus and Juliet do not meet again for several months.

Jot down reasons why you think Shakespeare might have made changes. Discuss your ideas with others explaining why the changes are necessary and important to a dramatic retelling of the story.

▣ Use your time line of the events in *Romeo and Juliet* as the basis for creating a boardgame. Working with a partner or within a small group, design a game board, playing pieces and any other items you might need to play the game, such as 'Chance' or 'Fate' cards.

Write a set of clear instructions for playing which will accompany your game. In preparing these consider the ages of those most likely to participate. Will the game be suitable for younger students, for people of your own age or for 'children of all ages'? Make sure that the language you use in your instructions is appropriate for its intended audience.

▣ Use your time line as the basis and inspiration for producing a ten-minute *Romeo and Juliet*. You will need to consider:
- the most important events and moments of the play that you want to include;

- whether to use selected lines from the play or to summarise speeches in your own words;
- how to show the passage of time;
- what to leave out;
- whether to have a chorus or narrator figure.

You may either improvise or script your play.

4 Use your time line as the basis for re-writing *Romeo and Juliet* as a mini-saga. (Mini-sagas first appeared as a competition in the *Sunday Telegraph Magazine*.) This is a story of *exactly* fifty words, although you can help yourself a bit by including a title of up to fifteen more words. You can do this alone or with a partner: either way, it's a challenge!

5 If newspapers had been published in Renaissance Italy then many parts of the story of Romeo and Juliet would surely have hit the headlines. In Shakespeare's time, they might have become immortalised in a broadsheet ballad (poems which were written about recent events, printed and sold in the street for a few pennies, usually rather sensational in nature).

Which of the events of the play would make good headline news or broadsheet ballads? Select some of your ideas and do one of the following:

- produce (on a desk-top publisher if you have access to one) a series of newspaper reports and editorials;
- write or improvise a series of radio or TV news reports (taping or videoing them if you can);
- compose your own broadsheet ballad (you may have to do some research on the ballad form before you do this, but ballads are easy to find).

6 In the final scene of the play Prince Escalus and the parents of Romeo and Juliet begin to piece together the events that have led up to the premature deaths of the two young lovers. Friar Lawrence and Balthasar are asked to reveal what they know and Romeo's letter to his father corroborates their words.

If the Prince were to conduct a full investigation into their deaths, he might require a number of documents as evidence of what has happened. Put together a suitable case file of documents including any or all of the following papers:

- the guest list for Capulet's masked ball (Act 1, scene 2, lines 65–73);
- Tybalt's letter to Romeo (Act 2, scene 4, lines 6–13);
- the marriage contract drawn up between Capulet and Count Paris (Act 1, scene 2; Act 3, scene 4);
- Friar Lawrence's letters to Romeo (Act 4, scene 1, lines 113–117: Act 5, scene 2, lines 18–20);
- Romeo's letter to his father (Act 5, scene 1, line 25; Act 5, scene 3, lines 275, 286–90);
- eye-witness accounts of the brawls in Act 1, scene 1; Act 3, scene 1;
- statements made by Friar Lawrence, the Nurse and Balthasar.

Before creating these documents you will need to gather careful evidence, not just from the parts of the text where they are mentioned or suggested, but also from other relevant scenes. Try to ensure that you write each in the most appropriate style.

Characters

Shakespeare does not usually give anything more than brief physical descriptions of his characters. As *Romeo and Juliet* begins we know very little about them except their relationship to one another from the list of characters before the text. What we learn about the appearance and personalities of the characters in Shakespeare's plays, comes entirely from their own speech and actions, or from the things that other characters say about them.

Romeo

🔲 Look closely at the following lines, in which Romeo's father talks about him:

MONTAGUE
  Many a morning hath he there been seen,

With tears augmenting the fresh morning's dew,
Adding to clouds more clouds with his deep sighs;
But all so soon as the all-cheering sun
Should in the farthest east begin to draw
The shady curtains from Aurora's bed,
Away from light steals home my heavy son,
And private in his chamber pens himself,
Shuts up his windows, locks fair daylight out,
And makes himself an artificial night.
Black and portentous must this humour prove,
Unless good counsel may the cause remove.

BENVOLIO
    My noble uncle, do you know the cause?

MONTAGUE
    I neither know it, nor can learn of him.

                                (Act 1, scene 1, lines 129–42)

List what you have learnt about Romeo from these lines. Remember that they are spoken before we ever see Romeo on stage. How do you think we are meant to feel about his character at this point?

2 Make a character map of Romeo, surrounding his name or a picture of him with adjectives or phrases which describe his character, based on what you have learnt about him from the short passage above. For example:

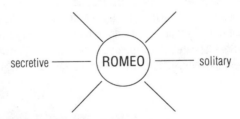

You can continue to add to this as you consider other parts of this scene. You could also add to your map the quotations and line references which give you the information.

328

▣ Make a detailed study of Romeo's character, paying particular attention to his mood changes and behaviour as the play progresses. Look closely at what other characters say about him and how his experiences affect him. Record your initial findings as a chart to help you with analysis later on:

Act/sc/line	Speaker	Mood/action	Character detail
2: 1: 14–19	Mercutio	Moping	Dying for love of Rosaline. Weak, not showing any heroic qualities.

▣ When you have completed Assignment 3, write a detailed character description of Romeo, with particular reference to any changes you note in him. Give evidence from the text, in the form of quotations or close references to details, to support your ideas, using act, scene and line numbers.

▣ O I am fortune's fool. (Act 3, scene 1, line 136)

Is he? There is a strong idea in the play that destiny or fate controls the characters' lives. On the other hand how much is Romeo to blame for the things that happen to him and to those around him in the play?

Hold a trial in which Romeo is placed in the dock. Present a case for his defence and for his prosecution.

Juliet

▣ Thirteen-year-old Juliet is possibly the most endearing character of the play. She seems to be attractive to look at, intelligent and thoughtful. Find lines from the play which help us to form this impression of her and record them on a character chart as you did for Romeo in Assignment 2 on page 328.

▣ When you have completed Assignment 6 write a character description of Juliet.

8 Juliet seems to be much more mature than the average thirteen-year-old girl. Do you agree with this, and if so does this mean that her character is unconvincing? Give quotations and references to support your views.

9 Describe Juliet's relationship with her Nurse. How and why does this relationship change as the play progresses?

10 Juliet is never seen with any friends of her own age. With a partner role-play a situation where she tells a friend or a cousin of her secret love for Romeo, and her feelings about the difficult situation she is in.

Friar Lawrence and the Nurse

11 Friar Lawrence's role in the play seems to be as one of the catalysts to the action. Without him Romeo and Juliet would not have been able to marry, nor attempt to get out of the predicament they find themselves in after Tybalt's death. In a similar way, the Nurse's assistance in conveying messages between the two lovers is essential to the drama. Both of these characters could be called mentors, as they offer friendship, help and advice.

If Romeo and Juliet were modern teenagers, they would be unlikely to turn to a monk and a nanny for help and advice. Working in groups role-play situations in which modern lovers seek advice from someone older than themselves. Who would their modern-day mentors be?

12 Find an example for a) Friar Lawrence and b) the Nurse when the advice they give is taken and acted upon by either Romeo or Juliet. Discuss whether you think the advice was good and whether the lovers were right to take it.

In contrast find an occasion when the advice given by the Friar and the Nurse is ignored or rejected. Decide whether the lovers would have been less unlucky if they had followed it. What might the consequences have been?

13 Is Romeo's relationship with Friar Lawrence in any way similar to that between Juliet and her Nurse? How would you describe Juliet's relationship with Friar Lawrence?

14 The deaths of Romeo and Juliet are to be investigated by the court of Verona at an inquest. Because of their part in the events leading up to the tragedy the Nurse and Friar Lawrence are to be called as the key witnesses.

Conduct the inquest with the following parts being played by members of your class or group:

- the coroner (this could, of course, be Prince Escalus himself)
- one or two lawyers to question the witnesses
- the Nurse
- Friar Lawrence
- other witnesses: decide before you begin who might be needed to give evidence
- a panel of jurors

You may also need to examine documents which are relevant to the case. Use the ones from the case file you compiled in Assignment 6 on pages 326–7.

Remember that the Nurse and the Friar are not on trial for a crime. An inquest tries only to establish the course of events leading up to an unusual or violent death and whether or not any crime has been committed.

Write the coroner's report from the inquest that has taken place. What was your final verdict? Outline in the report who, if anyone, was to blame for the deaths of the two lovers. What evidence was revealed to support this? Should they be brought to trial and if so what sentence would you recommend? In writing the report try to use language which would show consideration towards the families of the bereaved.

Other characters

15 Romeo's cousin, Benvolio and the dashing Mercutio, apart from being Romeo's close friends, are important characters in their own right particularly at the start of the play when we learn a great deal about Romeo from their conversations. They play active roles and have an impact on events. Good friends they may be but they are alike as chalk and cheese.

With reference to the text, prepare a comparison between Benvolio and Mercutio.

16 Benvolio, who began this bloody fray? (line 151)

In Act 3, scene 1, Benvolio is asked by Prince Escalus to describe what has happened. Where else has he been given this responsibility? Explain why Benvolio is called on to do this and what it tells us about his character.

17 Lady Capulet objects to Benvolio's report of the fight and says:

He is a kinsman to the Montague.
Affection makes him false; he speaks not true.
Some twenty of them fought in this black strife,

(Act 3, scene 1, lines 176–8)

Examine in detail Benvolio's report (lines 152–175) and decide whether the language of it is in any way biased towards Romeo's cause. Is Lady Capulet justified in her criticism? Discuss how a Capulet might tell the same story.

Write a speech for a kinsman of Tybalt to speak in place of Benvolio.

18 Mercutio's death comes as rather a shock to us in the course of events. Some critics have suggested that Shakespeare needed to dispose of Mercutio at this point in the play because he was becoming far more likeable than the hero, Romeo. What do you make of this suggestion? Write an alternative plot showing how the events of the play might change if Mercutio were to recover from his wounds.

19 Epitaphs are the words inscribed on the tomb of a dead person. Often they take the form of short poems. Write suitable epitaphs, in verse or prose, for the tombs of Mercutio and Tybalt.

20 Although the audience only ever sees the fiery side of Tybalt whenever he appears in the play, he is clearly much-loved by his relatives. Look back over the text and write a description based on your impressions of him. Is there anything about him at all that makes you feel some empathy towards him?

21 Although both sets of parents are important to the plot of *Romeo and Juliet* we see much less of Romeo's parents than of Juliet's. Because of this we have to guess at their characters as a whole from their brief appearances.

With a partner, work out what might be said in the following situations, and how you think the Montagues would react:

- Benvolio tells Lord Montague that Romeo is not sick but just in love with Rosaline.
- Benvolio tells Lady Montague that Romeo has been banished.
- Romeo confides in either one of his parents that he is in love with Juliet Capulet.

Support your views with references to the text.

22 What are your first impressions of Lord Capulet? Is he a likeable man? Do your ideas about him change as the play moves on?

Write a character study of Lord Capulet, focusing on the way in which Shakespeare reveals a little of his character at a time.

23 *Either* ask someone to take the role of Lord Capulet and put them in the hot seat *or* write his replies to the following questions:

- Why did you insist upon arranging Juliet's marriage?
- Why were you angry when she refused Paris, even though you had earlier said 'My will to her consent is but a part'?

- What were your reasons for bringing the day of the wedding forward?
- Your language towards Juliet was very unkind and unfair. How could you say such things to your only surviving child?
- How can your prove to us that you really did love her?

24 Lady Capulet's attitude towards Juliet also seems rather callous: 'I would the fool were married to her grave!' Is she a cruel mother? How far is her attitude towards Juliet based on her own experiences or the fact that she is quite young herself (around twenty-seven)? Write Lady Capulet's own explanation for this outburst.

Themes and ideas

Fate

Many of the things which we consider to be tragic have been brought about by chance happenings. We say that people have been unlucky, that Fate was unkind. In Shakespeare's plays, the tragedies in particular, ill-luck is not always entirely random: Othello's tragedy is caused by his own jealousy, Macbeth's is brought about by his uncontrollable ambition. Romeo and Juliet, however are seen as victims of circumstance affected by things beyond their control.

The Elizabethans believed, as do many people still today, in predestination – that the stars ruled their lives and that what was going to happen to them had been predetermined at the moment of their conception.

1 *Romeo and Juliet* is full of references to fortune or Fate. We are told immediately in the prologue that the lovers are 'star-crossed' and that their love is 'death-marked'. Look up these references to fortune in Act 3 of the play and make your own additions to the list:

- scene 1, line 119
- scene 1, line 136
- scene 5, lines 60–4

2. Which events in the play would you consider to be purely chance happenings? Look at your list of references and decide whether any of the events that Romeo and Juliet blame upon fortune are in fact the result of deliberate actions by themselves or others? (Refer back also to Assignment 5 on page 329 where you examined Romeo's part in events.)

3. Imagine that the letter from Friar Lawrence had got through to Romeo in Mantua. How would the story have ended? Write either an alternative final scene from Romeo's entrance in line 22, or a prose version.

Love

4. Do you believe that Romeo and Juliet could truly fall in love as quickly as they seem to in this play? How could actors convince their audiences without appearing trite and sentimental?

Rehearse a reading of the palmer's sonnet (Act 1, scene 5, lines 93–106) in pairs. Think carefully what the words mean in an attempt to make it as believable as possible.

5. What is the Nurse's attitude towards love? With reference to the text, compare her attitude with that of one other character either in discussion or as a piece of writing.

In performance

It is most important to bear in mind as you read *Romeo and Juliet* that it is a play and whenever possible you should attempt dramatic readings or performance of it. Look out for productions near your home, in the cinema or on television.

1. Design and build in miniature one or more sets for selected scenes of the play. Reading the information about the theatre buildings of Shakespeare's day in the 'Introduction' on page xii might help you with ideas for this.

2. It is common for *Romeo and Juliet* to be produced as if it were taking place in a time other than the Renaissance and a country other than Italy.

In a group discuss alternative times and locations, and design costumes that would fit one of these periods in history. Some research will be necessary. Write a justification for using the period of history you have chosen to accompany your costume drawings.

3 If you were asked to produce a new version of the play and could have your pick of any actors and actresses of your choice, who would you choose? Decide who you would cast in each role of the play and say what qualities the actor or actress has that makes him/her particularly suitable for the part.

4 Perform some of the scenes from the play yourselves, for your class, year group or whole school. Prepare a resume to show your audience how your chosen scene fits into the play as a whole.

5 If you are lucky enough to watch a production or film of the play, write a review of it. Focus particularly on how the actors choose to portray their roles: are they as you imagined? How well does the setting and lighting convey the times and places in which the events take place? If you can see two different performances, write a comparison of them.

6 Write or improvise the following missing scenes from the play or come up with an idea of your own:
- Benvolio's early morning sighting of Romeo;
- Rosaline's rejection of Romeo;
- The wedding of Romeo and Juliet;
- The incident where Friar John is unable to deliver the letter.

7 Write or improvise a modern-day version of the Romeo and Juliet story, using characters with which we would all be familiar and events which could happen to any of us. What part will luck play in your version?

Language

Romeo and Juliet is a play full of puns and word play. In Shakespeare's time this kind of wit was much admired: Mercutio calls Romeo a 'sure wit' and pretends that he cannot keep up with his jokes because his 'wits faint'.

■ Look back at the puns in the play and discuss whether it is true to say that they deal with particular topics or ideas. At what points in the scenes do puns appear? Is there a pattern? Are puns strictly limited to jokey characters? Try to decide why Shakespeare uses so many of these jokes in a play that is essentially a tragedy.

■ Puns are still used today in our modern sense of humour even if they tend to raise a groan. Make a collection of puns, writing down ones you hear and gathering together ones you see written down (newspaper headlines and advertising are both good sources). Display them in a suitable way and decide whether any of the subject matter has anything in common with the puns made by Shakespeare. You may be surprised at what you find.

■ When Lady Capulet talks to Juliet about Paris she compares him to a book. Romeo frequently refers to himself as if he were a ship sailing on the ocean. This is called using metaphor.

Find examples of imagery of this kind, where Romeo talks of himself as a ship. Make a note of them and then decide why this metaphor is particularly appropriate for Romeo and the events of the play.

Further assignments

■ Why does Rosaline never actually appear in the play?

- Role play a meeting between Rosaline and Romeo in which he tells her of his love and she rejects him.
- Write a series of letters between Romeo and Rosaline.

■ ... never was a story of more woe
Than this of Juliet and her Romeo.

Write an inscription to be placed on the plinth of statues in memory of Romeo and Juliet.

3 Read Shakespeare's *Othello* and write a comparison of the roles of Fate in the plays.

4 What part does acting rashly and hastily play in both *Othello* and *Romeo and Juliet*?

5 Read Shakespeare's *Much Ado About Nothing* and compare it with *Romeo and Juliet* in one of the following ways:

- Which pair of lovers in *Much Ado About Nothing* most resembles Romeo and Juliet, and why?
- Compare Juliet with Hero. In what ways are they similar? Could Hero's character ever be as tragic as Juliet's?

6 Read the first act of *King Lear*. In what ways does Lear's behaviour towards Cordelia resemble that of Lord Capulet? What do you think Shakespeare is trying to say about the love between fathers and daughters in general in either or both of these plays?

7 Watch either a production or film of *West Side Story*.

- How close is the plot of the film to that of *Romeo and Juliet*?
- Apart from Tony (for Romeo) and Maria (for Juliet) which other characters do you recognise? How similar are they to Shakespeare's characters?
- Do you think the conflict between the Jets and the Sharks is a good replacement for a family feud? Why?

8 Read Joan Lingard's *Across the Barricades*.

- What similarities can you see between this book and Shakespeare's play?
- Write your own short story, based on the plot of *Romeo and Juliet*, but set in modern times and in a place familiar to you.

Study questions

Many of the activities you have already completed (pages 311–37: before, during and after reading the play) will help you to answer the following questions. Before you begin to write, consider these points about essay writing:

- Spend some time deciding exactly what the essay question is asking. It may be useful to break the sentence down into phrases or words and decide what each part means.

- Focusing on the areas you have decided are relevant, note down as many quotations or references to the play as you can think of which are relevant to the answer.

- Decide on a shape which you think will be appropriate for the essay. It may be useful to think of a literal shape which will suit the argument.

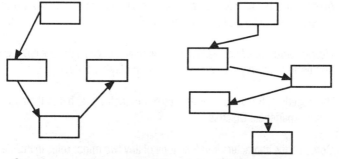

- Organise your ideas and quotations into sections to fit your shape; you could do this by placing notes into different piles.

- Write a first draft of your essay.

- Redraft as many times as you need to, taking care to consider the following:
  Does this answer the question?
  Is this essay easy to read, with clear organisation in which one point flows on to another?

Do the opening and concluding paragraphs seem clear and linked to the question set?

Are there any spelling or grammatical errors? Use a dictionary and thesaurus.

1 How important is Friar Lawrence to the play and what is his major dramatic function?

2 Examine the part played by comic characters in *Romeo and Juliet*.

3 'Wisely and slow. They stumble that run fast.'
Is *Romeo and Juliet* proof of this old adage?

4 *Romeo and Juliet* is always thought of as a play about love. What part does hate play in the downfall of the two lovers?

5 At the end of the play Romeo and Juliet's parents are reconciled. Do you consider this to be a satisfactory ending?

6 *Romeo and Juliet* has been popular with audiences since the day it was first performed. In your opinion is it still a play for today?

7 The tragedy of Romeo and Juliet lies not in their stars, but in their youth and inexperience. Discuss.

8 Compare the characters and functions of any two minor roles in the play.

9 The conflict between youth and age is forever present in *Romeo and Juliet*. Does youth triumph in the end?

Using part of the text

Below are two suggestions for using just a part of the text of *Romeo and Juliet*. You do not need to have read or seen the whole play in order to complete them.

▨ Love At First Sight

- Make up a tape of current love songs from the charts. Working as a whole class carry out the following simulated role-play.

- Pretend you are at a fancy dress party and dance in couples around the room playing the music in the background. One person must operate the tape. Stop the tape from time to time and when the music stops one couple speaks a chat-up line and a response that might be used in the present day. Keep stopping and starting the music so that every couple gets the chance to speak.

- Now select one person to be Romeo and one to be Juliet. Role play the party and then have the couple see each other across the crowded room, and move towards each other in the dancing. They meet, Romeo takes Juliet's hand. They begin to dance.

- Now add in another action. Select a character to play Tybalt, an angry young man, and one to play Capulet whose party it is. Tybalt sees Romeo, is angry and goes to tell Capulet that this is an enemy who has gate-crashed the party. Capulet tries to calm him down but Tybalt storms out.

- In a third run-through of the scene add in some other details: Capulet welcoming guests to the party and making jokes, instructing servants what to do, and guests dancing together. The end of the scene where Romeo and Juliet realise they have fallen in love with someone from an enemy family.

- Now read through Act 1, scene 5 of the play and see how close to the play your role-play has been. You could act out the scene ad-libbing lines or having learnt some of the words by heart.

- Imagine that the two lovers meet again later that night outside Juliet's bedroom window. Write a script of the scene.
- Now read Act 2, scene 2. How close was your script to what actually happened when they met again?

2 A Fight To The Death

Romeo and Juliet's love upsets many people in the play because they are from rival families.

- Read through Act 3, scene 1 of the play in which Mercutio, Romeo's friend, gets into a fight with Tybalt, Juliet's cousin, and both characters end up dead.
- Act out the scene using the actual words or ad-libbing what is said.
- Imagine Tybalt and Mercutio had not fought but had written angry letters to the prince instead. Write the letters including the words they would have said to get their point across.

There are many fight scenes in Shakespeare's plays. You could look at some of these and carry out the same tasks as those listed above. You could look out for:

Act 5, scene 7 of *Macbeth* where Macbeth must fight Macduff, the man he most fears.

Act 4, scene 4 of *Henry V* where Pistol fights a French soldier.

Study programme for Key Stage 3

Plot

1 Work in groups of four or five. Each group should take responsibility for one Act of the play. For your Act, add the details to this table under each heading. Work on a large sheet of paper and prepare to present your ideas to the rest of the class. Charts for each Act might then be displayed around your classroom as a reminder of the key events, characters and mood of each scene.

Act:

scene	place	main characters	main event	mood

2 Working in pairs, devise a flow-chart which places the main events of the play in the correct order. It should all fit onto one side of A4 paper. Compare your chart with that of another pair. Then keep this for reference as you work on the play.

3 Act 3 of a Shakespeare play is often thought of as a turning point. Look back at Act 3 (you might refer to the chart your class made) and then:

- Imagine you are a) Romeo, and b) Juliet, at the beginning

of Act 4. How has your situation changed since the beginning of Act 2? You might like to consider your relationship with your family and others, thoughts about your future, and your mood at this point.

- Now make a list, for each character, of the main events which have affected you. Which events occur in both lists?

■ Although **Romeo and Juliet** is classed as a tragedy, it contains a number of comic scenes. Examine these comments from critics who attempt to explain the function of the comedy.

- 'The comic scenes are important. They provide a break in the tension, allowing the audience to relax and to enjoy some comic relief.'

- 'Shakespeare only included comedy to entertain the uneducated people with some feeble puns and rude jokes. The play would really be better without it.' (See 'Introduction', page xii.)

- 'The comic scenes play a vital part in stressing the key themes of the play: we laugh at the foolish behaviour of lovers, as well as seeing the tragic results it can lead to.'

Now choose two of the following scenes and for each one discuss which of the quotations best applies. Be prepared to explain your decision. Why do you think Shakespeare included no comic scenes after Act 3 scene 1?

- Act 1, scene 1
- Act 1, scene 3
- Act 1, scene 4
- Act 2, scene 1
- Act 2, scene 4
- Act 2, scene 5

5   For never was a story of more woe
        Than this of Juliet and her Romeo

                           (Act 5, scene 3, lines 309–10)

After the play's tragic ending, do you think the audience would leave the theatre feeling depressed? Which events of the play should make us feel positive about human nature? Make a list of some ways in which Verona is a better place at the end of the play than it was at the beginning.

Characters

Romeo

1   What qualities do you look for in a hero? How many of these does Romeo have? Look at his behaviour at different points in the play and discuss how his qualities as a hero develop.

2   After killing Tybalt, Romeo says 'O, I am fortune's fool'. Trace Romeo's changing fortunes throughout the play, using a chart like the one below. Use the key to show what has happened to him.

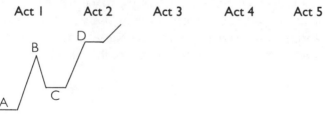

A = Romeo is moping because of his love for Rosaline
B = Romeo falls in love with Juliet
C = Romeo is told that Juliet is a member of the Capulet family
D =

3 Write Romeo's obituary as if you were either Benvolio or Friar Lawrence. What impression of Romeo would you wish to give?

Juliet

4 Imagine that Juliet keeps a diary. Write entries for the day she a) first met Romeo, and b) married him.

5 Compare Juliet's relationships with her mother and her Nurse. Working in threes, devise a role-play in which the two characters are interviewed about their relationships with Juliet. You should include questions about how the relationships developed during her final days.

Other characters

6 Discuss the qualities you look for in friends. Which of these do Benvolio and Mercutio share? How do the two friends differ?

7 Imagine that the Nurse is interviewed by Lord and Lady Capulet about the events leading up to their daughter's death and the part she played in them. Use your time-chart to locate those scenes in which the Nurse appears. You might present the interview to the rest of the group.

8 The Nurse enjoys talking! Select three or four short quotations which best represent different sides of her personality. You might present these on a poster or collage.

9 Look again at the scenes in which Friar Lawrence appears. Discuss whether you think he behaves responsibility.

[10] Imagine Friar Lawrence facing his Abbot (the head of his monastery). He must explain his part in the events of the play. In pairs, role-play two scenes: one in which the Abbot is sympathetic to the Friar's behaviour; the other in which he is sharply critical.

Dramatic effect

[1] *Romeo and Juliet* has been performed in many different types of theatre. Imagine that you are going to put on a production of the play at your school. What kind of performance space do you have, if any?

- theatre in-the-round (audience on all sides);
- thrust stage (audience on three sides);
- proscenium arch stage (audience directly facing the stage).

Discuss how you might use this space to present one of the following scenes. What are the problems that you would encounter? Use diagrams to show your ideas.

a) opening street-fight (Act 1, scene 1)
b) balcony scene (Act 2, scene 2)
c) Friar Lawrence's cell (Act 2, scene 6)
d) the Capulet vault (Act 5, scene 3)

[2] Choose one of the following scenes. Select the moment of greatest dramatic interest and produce a freeze-frame to represent the action. Others in the class might then guess which scene you are portraying, and ask you about the decisions you have made.

- the fight between Mercutio and Tybalt (Act 3, scene 1);
- Juliet's argument with her parents (Act 3, scene 5);
- the events in the vault (Act 5, scene 3).

3 'Dramatic irony' is the effect created when the audience knows something that a character does not – for example, in pantomimes when the audience shouts out 'He's behind you!' Look at these points in the play and make a table which shows a) what the character knows, and b) what the audience knows.

- Tybalt challenging Romeo (Act 3, scene 1);
- Lady Capulet talking to Juliet (Act 3, scene 5);
- Juliet talking to Paris (Act 4, scene 1);
- Juliet talking to her parents (Act 4, scene 2).

4 Choose one of the comic scenes in the play. Working in a group, prepare a performance of part of the scene. Think about how you will make the performance funny. Focus upon how characters should speak and behave, and practise getting the timing of the dialogue right.

5 Learn a solo speech from the play and prepare it for performance. Think about your tone of voice, pace, volume, use of pauses, posture and movement. You might keep a copy of the speech with your own handwritten notes on it. Then write the process of preparing the performance, explaining the decisions you made.

Style and language

1 In a group, discuss what your expectations of reading Shakespeare were before you started *Romeo and Juliet*. Then look back at the Chorus' Prologue on page 7. What features of the style might make the speech difficult for people who are not familiar with Shakespeare? Find an example for each of the following:

- unusual word-order;
- unfamiliar vocabulary;
- words which we no longer use;
- poetic language.

2 Sometimes in a speech Shakespeare uses word patterns to stress a certain mood or theme. Look closely at the Prince's speech on page 19. Pick out words which could be placed under the following headings (some words might fit under more than one heading):

- anger/hatred;
- violence;
- wrong-doing.

Now in a group of four, one person reads the speech aloud whilst each of the others echoes the words from one of the lists. Practise reading the speech like this, so that you emphasise the Prince's mood and meaning.

3 Read the section on *images* in the 'Introduction' (page xix). Shakespeare often gets us to understand a feeling or idea by making a comparison with something else. Choose a key speech (you might use the Prince's speech from the previous activity). Then pick out three quotations which show the use of imagery, using the following table to show how they work:

quotation	idea/subject	compared with	effect
'fire of your pernicious rage' (1:1:82)	rage	fire	shows power of their hatred

4 Read page xviii of the 'Introduction' (prose, rhyme, blank verse). Look again at Act 1, scene 3.

- Which form is used for the Nurse's speech?
- Which is used for most of Lady Capulet's speech?
- Where in the scene is rhyming verse used?

Now discuss why Shakespeare might have used these forms in this way?

5 Look at Juliet's speech (Act 4, scene 3). In pairs, practise reading this aloud in different ways:

- one person should read the speech, a line at a time, emphasising its rhythm;
- the other should repeat each line, trying to make it sound like normal speech;
- finally, both read the whole speech aloud at the same time, each using the different style you have been practising.

If you were performing this speech, how far would you emphasise the rhythm?

Test questions

Read the following extract from Act 1, scene 5 of **Romeo and Juliet**.

ROMEO
  (*To himself*) O she doth teach the torches to burn bright!
  It seems she hangs upon the cheek of night   45
  As a rich jewel in an Ethiop's ear;
  Beauty too rich for use, for earth too dear.
  So shows a snowy dove trooping with crows,
  As yonder lady o'er her fellows shows.
  The measure done, I'll watch her place of stand,   50
  And, touching hers, make blessèd my rude hand.
  Did my heart love till now? Forswear it, sight,
  For I ne'er saw true beauty till this night.

TYBALT
  This, by his voice, should be a Montague.
  Fetch me my rapier, boy. (*Exit page*) What dares the slave   55
  Come hither, covered with an antic face,
  To fleer and scorn at our solemnity?
  Now, by the stock and honour of my kin,
  To strike him dead, I hold it not a sin.

CAPULET
  Why, how now, kinsman! Wherefore storm you so?   60

TYBALT
  Uncle, this is a Montague, our foe;
  A villain that is hither come in spite,
  To scorn at our solemnity this night.

CAPULET
  Young Romeo is it?

TYBALT
                'T is he, that villain, Romeo.

Section A

1 Explain the meaning of the following words and phrases as
   they are used in the extract:
   a) 'antic face' (line 56)
   b) 'by the stock and honour of my kin' (line 58)
   c) 'storm' (line 60)

2 Where does this scene take place? How has Romeo come to
   be there and who is with him?

3 a) Why is Tybalt so angry? How typical is his behaviour in this
      scene of his actions in the play as a whole?
   b) In a performance, what else would be happening on stage
      as Tybalt and Capulet speak to each other?

4 How does Capulet go on to react to what Tybalt tells him?
   How does this affect later events in the play?

Section B

1 Towards the end of the play the Prince says to Capulet and
   Montague:

       See what a scourge is laid upon your hate,
       That heaven finds means to kill your joys with love.

   Do you agree with him? Explain your reasons.

2 The last two lines of the play are:

> For never was a story of more woe
> Than this of Juliet and her Romeo.

What elements in the play prevent **Romeo and Juliet** from being a story *only* of woe?

3 In what ways does friendship play a part in **Romeo and Juliet**?

4 Write about *one* of the following characters. Try to explain his/her function in the play.

a) Friar Lawrence b) Nurse c) Capulet

5 How far is each of the following characters responsible for the tragic outcome of the play?

a) Tybalt b) Capulet c) Mercutio

6 Look at the photographs from the play on pages 354–6. Put the photographs in the correct order in which they would appear in the play.

Now turn to page 357. Match each quotation with the appropriate photograph.

Photograph A

(Royal Shakespeare Company 1983, © Donald Cooper, Photostage)

Photograph B

(Royal Shakespeare Company 1991, © Donald Cooper, Photostage)

Photograph C

(Royal Shakespeare Company,
© The Panic Pictures Library)

Match each of these quotations with the photographs A, B and C:

I   Even or odd, of all the days in the year come Lammas-Eve at night shall she be fourteen. Susan and she – God rest all Christian souls – were of an age.

2   I am hurt.
    A plague o' both your houses!

3   O my love, my wife!
    Death, that hath sucked the honey of thy breath,
    Hath had no power yet upon thy beauty.

Longman Group UK Limited,
Longman House, Burnt Mill, Harlow,
Essex CM20 2JE, England
and Associated Companies throughout the world.

© Longman Group UK Limited 1994

First published 1992
This hardback edition first published 1994

Editorial material set in 10/12 point Helvetica Light Condensed
Produced by Longman Singapore (Pte) Ltd
Printed and bound in Great Britain by
Butler & Tanner Ltd, Frome and London

ISBN 0 582 24591 5

Cover illustration by Reg Cartwright

The Publisher's policy is to use paper manufactured from sustainable forests.

Longman Literature
Series editor: Roy Blatchford

Novels

Jane Austen   *Pride and Prejudice*   0 582 07720 6
Charlotte Brontë   *Jane Eyre*   0 582 07719 2
Emily Brontë   *Wuthering Heights*   0 582 07782 6
Charles Dickens   *Great Expectations*   0 582 07783 4
F Scott Fitzgerald   *The Great Gatsby*   0 582 06023 0
                         Tender is the Night   0 582 09716 9
Nadine Gordimer   *July's People*   0 582 06011 7
Graham Greene   *The Captain and the Enemy*   0 582 06024 9
Thomas Hardy   *Far from the Madding Crowd*   0 582 07788 5
                      Tess of the D'Urbervilles   0 582 09715 0
Aldous Huxley   *Brave New World*   0 582 06016 8
Robin Jenkins   *The Cone-Gatherers*   0 582 06017 6
Doris Lessing   *The Fifth Child*   0 582 06021 4
Joan Lindsay   *Picnic at Hanging Rock*   0 582 08174 2
Bernard Mac Laverty   *Lamb*   0 582 06557 7
Brian Moore   *Lies of Silence*   0 582 08170 X
George Orwell   *Animal Farm*   0 582 06010 9
                     Nineteen Eighty-Four   0 582 06018 4
Alan Paton   *Cry, the Beloved Country*   0 582 07787 7
Paul Scott   *Staying On*   0 582 07718 4
Virginia Woolf   *To the Lighthouse*   0 582 09714 2

Short Stories

Jeffrey Archer   *A Twist in the Tale*   0 582 06022 2
Susan Hill   *A Bit of Singing and Dancing*   0 582 09711 8
Bernard Mac Laverty   *The Bernard Mac Laverty Collection*   0 582 08172 6

Poetry

Five Modern Poets   edited by Barbara Bleiman   0 582 09713 4